DZOGCHEN
THE SELF-PERFECTED STATE

DZOGCHEN
THE SELF-PERFECTED STATE

Chögyal Namkhai Norbu

edited by
Adriano Clemente

and translated into English by
John Shane

Snow Lion Publications
Ithaca, New York

Snow Lion Publications
P.O. Box 6483
Ithaca, New York 14851 USA
607-273-8519

This edition published by arrangement with the Penguin Group.
Copyright © 1996 Namkhai Norbu
This translation copyright © 1996 John Shane

First English edition copyright © 1989 Namkhai Norbu
Translation copyright © 1989 John Shane
Originally published as *Dzogchen, Lo stato di autoperfezione,* a cura di
    Adriano Clemente, Rome 1986.

ISBN 1-55939-057-3

Library of Congress Cataloging-in-Publication Data

Namkhai Norbu, 1938-
    Dzogchen: the self-perfected state / Namkhai Norbu; edited
    by Adriano Clemente; and translated into English by John Shane.
        p. cm.
    Includes bibliographical references.
    ISBN 1-55939-057-3
    1. Rdzogs-chen (Rñiṅ-ma-pa) I. Clemente, Adriano II. Shane,
John. III. Title.
BQ7662.4.N336 1996
294.3'44—dc20   95-43615
                                                              CIP

CONTENTS

Note to the Cover Illustration

The illustration on the cover of this book is the central image of a thanka, or Tibetan scroll painting, executed by Glen Eddy, an American thanka painter trained in the traditional manner who has been painting thankas for twenty-four years.

The central figure of the thanka shows the author of this book, the Dzogchen master Chögyal Namkhai Norbu, seated in contemplation in a form befitting a great exponent of the tradition of the Mahasiddhas. His right hand is raised in the mudra or gesture of 'Direct Introduction', while his left hand presses on one of the points that enable a practitioner to control the flow of subtle energy in the body in order to favour the development of a particular aspect of practice.

Chögyal Namkhai Norbu is seen wearing the 'Onra', a kind of short trousers traditionally worn by practitioners of Yantra Yoga, a traditional system of Tibetan Yoga taught to Chögyal Namkhai Norbu by his uncle Togden Ogyen Tenzin, who accomplished the supreme realization of the rainbow body. Yantra Yoga uses movements as well as positions to enable the practitioner to coordinate and gain mastery of the prana, or subtle energy of the physical body, furthering the development of contemplation. Chögyal Namkhai Norbu has taught this system of Yoga to his students, and a comprehensive book on this subject is now being prepared for publication. Chögyal Namkhai Norbu is shown with a 'Melong', or small mirror, on a cord around his neck. The Melong is a symbol used in Dzogchen to explain the nature of the mind.

The original painting was sponsored by John Shane, and executed following the instructions of Chögyal Namkhai Norbu.

Frontispiece

Chögyal Namkhai Norbu at a retreat at Tsegyelgar Dzogchen Community, Conway, Massachusetts, November 1994. Photo by John Shane. Copyright © John Shane 1994.

Text Illustrations

Line Drawings by Glen Eddy
Refuge field copyright © Dzogchen Community in America. All other drawings copyright © Glen Eddy.

Appearing at the top centre is Samantabhadra, who represents the Dharmakaya. Vajrasattva and Vajrapani are shown below him to the left and right respectively, representing the Sambhogakaya, while Garab Dorje, their Nirmanakaya emanation, is below and between them. He was the first Dzogchen master to teach on this planet in this time cycle. The principal figure at the center of the refuge field is Padmasambhava or Guru Rinpoche, who is visualized as the union of all the masters from whom one has received transmission. In Dzogchen one takes Refuge in the Guru, the Deva, and the Dakini: below Padmasambhava to the left and right are the Heruka, or Deva, Guru Dragpo, and the Dakini Singhamukha, wrathful male and female meditational divinities. Below and between them is the principal Guardian of the Dzogchen teachings, Ekajati, while below her to the left and right respectively are two further Protectors of the teachings, Rahula and Dorje Legpa.

Chögyal Namkhai Norbu. Photo by John Shane.

TRANSLATOR'S NOTE

I began translating this book in Italy in the Spring of 1987, continued with the project while accompanying Namkhai Norbu Rinpoche on his summer teaching schedule across the United States, through Hawaii and Japan, and completed the work in Lhasa, Tibet, in October of the same year, when I had the good fortune to accompany Rinpoche on a visit to his native land and to see for the first time the country whose culture I had studied for so long. Just as I finished the translation the political situation in Lhasa erupted onto the front pages of the world's newspapers and television screens, raising the general public's level of awareness of Tibet's recent history, and promoting a wider understanding of the importance of Tibetan culture and of its present plight.

I hope to write a full account elsewhere of what I have experienced on my long journey to Tibet in Rinpoche's company, a journey to the heart of Tibet's culture undertaken in many lands other than Tibet, over many years of study and practice of the teachings explained in this book. What I want to say here, however, is how much finally arriving in Tibet itself, and seeing the situation as it really is there today, brought home to me the importance of grounding these precious teachings in the countries of the world where the freedom to teach and practice them without hindrance is enjoyed.

More than ever I feel a profound sense of gratitude to Namkhai Norbu Rinpoche for his continued patience in sharing his knowledge with us so generously, and for his untiring efforts to ensure that the living culture of his native country does not become extinct. Freedom at a political level is a great and important asset, as is freedom from hunger and disease; but true freedom is a spiritual quality, to be found within each individual. The teachings in this book point the way to such true freedom. May this translation serve to bring them to those who are open to them, wherever they may be.

John Shane
Lhasa, Tibet
October, 1987

Note to the Snow Lion edition

Looking back for a moment over the seven years that have passed since the first publication of this book, I marvel at how much Chögyal Namkhai Norbu has achieved in that time in so many different fields of activity: he has, among other things, written an extraordinary number of books of profound wisdom and scholarship, continued to give Dzogchen teachings literally all over the world, and brought much-needed practical and spiritual assistance to the people of Tibet.

Thinking of the selfless dedication with which he has, without thought of the cost to himself, unceasingly worked and traveled in order to bring benefit to others, I find tears of gratitude and devotion welling up in my eyes.

Earlier this year Rinpoche was unfortunately very ill indeed for a relatively short period of time, and we really feared we might lose him. But this new Snow Lion edition of one of his most accessible books goes to press at a particularly auspicious time: its illustrious author is, to the great joy of his many friends and students, once again well enough to resume his teaching activities.

I pray with all my heart that his health will continue to remain good and that his activities will long continue to benefit innumerable beings.

May all his plans and wishes be brought to completion!

John Shane
November 1995

A Note on Namkhai Norbu Rinpoche's title of 'Chögyal'

The title of 'Chögyal', meaning 'Dharmaraja', or 'Dharma King', is one of the titles accorded to Namkhai Norbu Rinpoche when he was recognized as a child by H.H. the Sixteenth Gyalwa Karmapa and other eminent Tibetan lamas as the mind incarnation of Pema Karpo, the great master who united a number of feuding Himalayan royal clans to found what is now the state of Bhutan. Pema Karpo and his later reincarnations became the temporal and spiritual rulers of that country, and thus despite the fact that Chögyal Namkhai Norbu himself has no political connections with Bhutan whatsoever and was himself born and raised in Tibet, his predecessors held, in relation to Bhutan, a rank similar to that which the Dalai Lamas held in Tibet. Namkhai Norbu Rinpoche has no aspirations in the political sphere, but as the mind reincarnation of Pema Karpo, he nevertheless holds the title and seals of the Chögyal, and manifests the spiritual aspect of his predecessors' activity in the changed conditions of the modern world.

As is more widely known, Chögyal Namkhai Norbu is also recognized as the reincarnation of the great Dzogchen master Adzam Drugpa, who lived in Tibet at the turn of the century. Adzam Drugpa was also a reincarnation of Pema Karpo, and it is thus considered that the mind streams of the two separate simultaneous reincarnations that were emanated by Pema Karpo as the subsequent Dharmarajas of Bhutan and as Adzam Drugpo in Tibet are now re-united in the person of Chögyal Namkhai Norbu.

EDITOR'S INTRODUCTION

The Dzogchen *(rdzogs chen)*[1] teachings, according to the master Namkhai Norbu Rinpoche, can be useful to everyone to enable them to discover their own true condition and at the same time to help them to learn to live their lives in a relaxed manner. We will discover in the pages of this book what is meant by "relaxation" in Dzogchen, and how it is possible to "practice" without either renouncing anything, or having to commit oneself to any activities that might be incompatible with one's normal daily life.

Although, in the course of Tibet's history, Dzogchen was introduced and spread around the country by the two great traditions of Buddhism and Bon,[2] Dzogchen itself should not be classified as a religious or philosophical tradition. Rather it is a complete way of knowledge of the individual's state of being, beyond the limits of either religious belief or culture. Without ever having become a sect in itself, Dzogchen has remained a direct teaching because, over the course of the centuries, it has maintained a purity and authenticity of transmission incompatible with the more formal structures of religious institutions.

Buddhism was officially introduced to Tibet during the reign of King Trisong Detsen (Khri srong lDe brtsan) (742-797 AD), although there had for centuries already been influxes of Buddhist culture from India, from China, and from other neighbouring countries. Trisong Detsen invited to his court Buddhist masters and pandits from India, and from Oddiyana, an ancient kingdom which has been identified as having been located in the Swat Valley, in present-day Pakistan. Oddiyana, which is considered to have been the place where the tantric teachings originated, was in ancient times a country with a thriving Buddhist culture, and many masters went there to receive teachings. There too, Dzogchen, which was later incorporated into the Buddhist tradition, had its origin, with the master Garab Dorje (dGa' rab rDo rje), several centuries before the Christian era.[3] Garab Dorje's teaching, said to be "beyond the karmic law of cause and effect," turned the traditionalist views of his first disciples, who were famous Buddhist pandits, completely upside down. Because of this, from then on, the transmission of Dzogchen came to take place in secret, parallel to that of the official Buddhist doctrines.

Buddhism in its tantric form was principally introduced to Tibet by Padmasambhava, a master capable of miraculous activities, who came from his native Oddiyana at the invitation of King Trisong Detsen. With the aim of also furthering the spread of the Dzogchen teachings in Tibet, Padmasambhava suggested to the King that he send a Tibetan named Vairocana to Oddiyana. This latter received all the Dzogchen teachings at the feet of the master Shri Singha, disciple of Manjushrimitra,[4] who was in turn a disciple of Garab Dorje, and later introduced these teachings to Tibet, transmitting them only to a select few. The pandit Vimalamitra, also a disciple of Shri Singha, was subsequently invited to the king's court, where he transmitted further

Dzogchen teachings. This period of fervent activity of the spreading and translation of original Buddhist texts also saw the translation into Tibetan of Dzogchen texts, principally from the language of Oddiyana. All the texts translated in this period, whether containing tantric or Dzogchen teachings, were later classified as belonging to the "Ancient" tradition or Nyingmapa *(rNying ma pa)*, as distinct from the Tantras translated in the second spread of the teachings in the eleventh century.[5] Thus Dzogchen has come to be considered part of the doctrines of the Nyingmapa school of Tibetan Buddhism. In this tradition all the various systems of teaching are subdivided into nine paths or "vehicles" *(yāna)*. These are:

1. The worldly vehicle of divinities and men *('jig rten lha mi'i theg pa)*, which includes all non-Buddhist types of religious system.
2. The vehicle of the *shravakas* (listeners) and of the *pratyekabuddhas* (those who aspire for enlightenment just for themselves). This comprises the teachings of Hinayana Buddhism.
3. The vehicle of the *bodhisattvas*, which consists of the teachings of the Mahayana.
4. Kriya Tantra
5. Ubhava Tantra
6. Yoga Tantra
   These three vehicles are called "external Tantras," because the practices involved in them are principally based on purification and on preparing oneself to receive the wisdom of realized beings.
7. Mahayoga
8. Anuyoga
9. Atiyoga
   These are all generally known as "internal Tantras," but in fact only the first two are tantric teachings, the

principle of tantra being the transformation of the psycho-physical constituents of the individual into the pure dimension of realization. *Atiyoga,* which is synonymous with Dzogchen, is based on the path of self-liberation, and on the direct experiential knowledge of the primordial state. This subdivision of the Tantras is peculiar to the Nyingmapa school.

The other three main Tibetan Buddhist traditions, Kagyudpa *(bKa' rgyud pa),* Sakyapa *(Sa skya pa)* and Gelugpa *(dGe lugs pa)* classify the higher Tantras or *Anuttara Tantra* as follows:

1. Pitriyoga: Father Tantras.
2. Matriyoga: Mother Tantras.
3. Advityayoga: Non-dual Tantras.

All these three types of Anuttara-tantra are based on the system of gradual transformation, as is practiced in the *Mahayoga* of the Nyingmapa tradition. The *Anuyoga is* a system based on non-gradual transformation only found in the oldest tradition—the Nyingmapa.

The written Dzogchen teachings are divided into three sections: the Series of the Nature of the Mind *(sems sde),*[6] the Series of Primordial Space *(klong sde),* and the Series of Secret Instructions *(man ngag sde).* The first two of these were introduced into Tibet by Vairochana, the third by Vimalamitra. Those teachings that were originally transmitted by Padmasambhava and then hidden in various places in Tibet are also part of the Series of Secret Instructions. This kind of text, known as "terma" *(gter ma)* or "treasures,"[7] began to be rediscovered from the thirteenth century onwards. Those texts which, on the other hand, were transmitted orally from the time of Garab Dorje onwards, are known as the "oral tradition" *(bka' ma).*

Another tradition of Dzogchen teachings, differing both in its origin and the lineage of its masters, is to be found within the Bon religion, which spread from Shang-shung, an ancient kingdom of west Tibet.[8] Given the present state of research, it is impossible to know if there was one single point of origin of all the Dzogchen teachings. In the course of centuries, the Dzogchen teachings have been practiced by masters belonging to all the schools and traditions. This is because the very nature of Dzogchen transcends sectarian limits and man-made barriers.

Lineage holder in a line of masters that goes back to Garab Dorje himself, Chögyal Namkhai Norbu now teaches Dzogchen in the West. Born in 1938, near Derghe in eastern Tibet, from his childhood on he received many teachings and initiations from masters of various traditions, particularly from two of his uncles who were great practitioners of Dzogchen.[9] At the age of eight he began a college education that included many years' study of Buddhist philosophy, and of the various other branches of Tibetan knowledge. In 1954, upon completion of this course of studies, he was invited to go to China as part of a delegation representing the Buddhist monasteries of Tibet. There, he taught Tibetan for two years at Chengdu, in Sichuan province, on the western borders of China. During this period he had the opportunity of meeting Konkar Rinpoche (Gangs dkar rin po che) (1903-1956),[10] the famous master of the Kagyudpa tradition, from whom he received many teachings. But it was on his return to Tibet that he met, after a premonitory dream, the master who was to open the gates of knowledge for him, Rinzin Changchub Dorje (Rig 'dzin Byang chub rDo rje) (1826-1961), a great master of Dzogchen and discoverer of terma, who lived simply as a village doctor. Throughout the several months during which Namkhai Norbu Rinpoche stayed with this master, he received many essential

Dzogchen teachings, but above all he received transmission of the true state of knowledge of Dzogchen, which is beyond books and words. Rinzin Changchub Dorje continues to be a constant example and reference point in both the life and teachings of Namkhai Norbu Rinpoche.

In 1958 Chögyal Namkhai Norbu travelled to India to study and to visit various holy places. Unable to return to Tibet because of the political upheaval there, he went to Sikkhim, where he lived for two years. In 1960 Giuseppe Tucci invited him to Italy, to help with research at the Institute for Far and Middle Eastern Studies in Rome. Since 1964 he has been teaching Tibetan and Mongolian language and literature at the Oriental Institute of the University of Naples. During the last twenty years Chögyal Namkhai Norbu has undertaken an in-depth study of the origins of Tibetan culture, paying particular attention to the Bon tradition, the source of the culture of Shang-shung, and thus of Tibet. He has written several books on this subject which are extremely important for scholars of Tibetan history and culture.[11]

In 1976 he began to transmit Dzogchen teachings, first in Italy and then in other countries. His disciples form the "Dzogchen Community," whose reference point in Italy is situated on the slopes of Monte Amiata, near Arcidosso, in Tuscany, and is called Merigar. In the last few years Chögyal Namkhai Norbu has given seminars on Tibetan Yoga, medicine, and astrology in various parts of the world. In 1983 he presided over the first International Convention on Tibetan Medicine, held in Venice and Arcidosso.

This book is based principally on teachings given by Namkhai Norbu Rinpoche at Merigar in 1985 and 1986. I have divided the text into two parts, the first of which is made up of talks that clarify what the Dzogchen teachings are about, also explaining what distinguishes these teachings from other paths to realization. The second part, "The

Cuckoo of the State of Presence," is a commentary on the *Six Vajra Verses (rDo rje tshig drug)*, a very short text that sums up the essence of Dzogchen in six lines, which was transmitted in Oddiyana by Shri Singha to Vairochana. In the three chapters which form this second part Namkhai Norbu Rinpoche reveals, in a simple and nonintellectual manner, what we mean when we talk about the "practice" of Dzogchen.

It is my hope that these teachings will contribute to the awakening in mankind of a true and "nonconceptual" state of knowledge, beyond all conditioning.

Adriano Clemente

PART ONE

Chapter One
THE INDIVIDUAL:
BODY, VOICE, AND MIND

Someone who begins to develop an interest in the teachings can tend to distance themselves from the reality of material things, as if the teachings were something completely apart from daily life. Often, at the bottom of all this, there is an attitude of giving up and running away from one's own problems, with the illusion that one will be able to find something that will miraculously help one to transcend all that. But the teachings are based on the principle of our actual human condition. We have a physical body with all its various limits: each day we have to eat, work, rest, and so on. This is our reality, and we can't ignore it.

The Dzogchen teachings are neither a philosophy, nor a religious doctrine, nor a cultural tradition. Understanding the message of the teachings means discovering one's own true condition, stripped of all the self-deceptions and falsifications which the mind creates. The very meaning of the

Tibetan term Dzogchen, "Great Perfection," refers to the true primordial state of every individual and not to any transcendent reality.

Many spiritual paths have as their basis the principle of compassion, of benefiting others. In the Mahayana Buddhist tradition, for example, compassion is one of the fundamental points of the practice, together with the knowledge of the true nature of phenomena, or "voidness." Sometimes, however, compassion can become something constructed and provisional, because we don't understand the real principle of it. A genuine, not artificial, compassion, can only arise after we have discovered our own condition. Observing our own limits, our conditioning, our conflicts and so on, we can become truly conscious of the suffering of others, and then our own experience becomes a basis or model for being able to better understand and help those around us.

The only source of every kind of benefit for others is awareness of our own condition. When we know how to help ourselves and how to work with our situation we can really benefit others, and our feeling of compassion will arise spontaneously, without the need for us to hold ourselves to the rules of behaviour of any given religious doctrine.

What do we mean when we say, "becoming aware of our own true condition"? It means observing ourselves, discovering who we are, who we believe we are, and what our attitude is towards others and to life. If we just observe the limits, the mental judgments, the passions, the pride, the jealousy, and the attachments with which we close ourselves up in the course of one single day, where do they arise from, what are they rooted in? Their source is our dualistic vision, and our conditioning. To be able to help both ourselves and others we need to overcome all the limits in which we are enclosed. This is the true function of the teachings.

Every kind of teaching is transmitted through the culture and knowledge of human beings. But it is important not to confuse any culture or tradition with the teachings themselves, because the essence of the teachings is knowledge of the nature of the individual. Any given culture can be of great value because it is the means which enables people to receive the message of a teaching, but it is not the teaching itself. Let's take the example of Buddhism. Buddha lived in India, and to transmit his knowledge he didn't create a new form of culture, but used the culture of the Indian people of his time as the basis for communication. In the *Abhidharma-kosha*,[1] for example, we find concepts and notions, such as the description of Mount Meru and the five continents, which are typical of the ancient culture of India, and which should not be considered of fundamental importance to an understanding of the Buddha's teaching itself. We can see another example of this kind of thing in the completely novel form Buddhism took in Tibet after its integration with the indigenous Tibetan culture. In fact, when Padmasambhava introduced the Vajrayana into Tibet he did not do away with the ritual practices used by the ancient Bon tradition, but knew just how to use them, incorporating them into the Buddhist tantric practices.

If one doesn't know how to understand the true meaning of a teaching through one's own culture, one can create confusion between the external form of a religious tradition and the essence of its message. Let's take the example of a Western person interested in Buddhism, who goes to India looking for a teacher. There he meets a traditional Tibetan master who lives in an isolated monastery and knows nothing about Western culture. When such a master is asked to teach, he will follow the method he is used to using to teach Tibetans. But the Western person has some very big difficulties to overcome, beginning with the obstacle of language.

Perhaps he will receive an important initiation and will be struck by the special atmosphere, by the spiritual "vibration," but will not understand its meaning. Attracted by the idea of an exotic mysticism he may stay for a few months in the monastery, absorbing a few aspects of Tibetan culture and religious customs. When he returns to the West he is convinced that he has understood Buddhism and feels different from those around him, behaving just like a Tibetan.

But the truth is that for a Westerner to practice a teaching that comes from Tibet there is no need for that person to become like a Tibetan. On the contrary, it is of fundamental importance for him to know how to integrate that teaching with his own culture in order to be able to communicate it, in its essential form, to other Westerners. But often, when people approach an Eastern teaching, they believe that their own culture is of no value. This attitude is very mistaken, because every culture has its value, related to the environment and circumstances in which it arose. No culture can be said to be better than another; rather it depends on the human individual whether he or she will derive greater or lesser advantage from it in terms of inner development. For this reason it is useless to transport rules and customs into a cultural environment different from the one in which they arose.

A person's habits and cultural environment are of importance to that individual to enable them to understand a teaching. You can't transmit a state of knowledge using examples that are not known to the listener. If *tsampa*[2] with Tibetan tea is served to a Westerner, he or she will probably have no idea how to eat it. A Tibetan, on the other hand, who has eaten tsampa since he was a child, won't have that problem, and will right away mix the tsampa with tea and eat it. In the same way, if one does not have a knowledge of the culture through which a teaching is transmitted, it is difficult to understand its essential message. This is the value of knowing about a particular culture. But the teachings involve an inner state of knowledge which should not be confused with the culture through which it is transmitted, or with its habits, customs, political and social systems, and so on. Human beings have created different cultures in different times and places, and someone who is interested in the teachings must be aware of this and know how to work with different cultures, without however becoming conditioned by their external forms.

For example, those who already have a certain familiarity with Tibetan culture might think that to practice Dzogchen you have to convert to either Buddhism or Bon, because Dzogchen has been spread through these two religious traditions. This shows how limited our way of thinking is. If we decide to follow a spiritual teaching, we are convinced that it is necessary for us to change something, such as our way of dressing, of eating, of behaving, and so on. But Dzogchen does not ask one to adhere to any religious doctrine or to enter a monastic order, or to blindly accept the teachings and become a "Dzogchenist." All of these things can, in fact, create serious obstacles to true knowledge.

The fact is that people are so used to putting labels on everything that they are incapable of understanding anything that does not come within their limits. Let me give a personal example. Every now and then I will meet a Tibetan who doesn't know me well, and who will ask me the question, "Which school do you belong to?" In Tibet, over the course of the centuries, there have arisen four principal Tibetan Buddhist traditions, and if a Tibetan hears of a master, he is convinced that the master must necessarily belong to one of these four sects. If I reply that I am a practitioner of Dzogchen, this person will presume that I belong to the

Nyingmapa school, within which the Dzogchen texts have been preserved. Some people, on the other hand, as has actually happened, knowing that I have written some books on Bon with the aim of re-evaluating the indigenous culture of Tibet, would say that I am a Bonpo. But Dzogchen is not a school or sect, or a religious system. It is simply a state of knowledge which masters have transmitted beyond any limits of sect or monastic tradition. In the lineage of the Dzogchen teachings there have been masters belonging to all social classes, including farmers, nomads, nobles, monks, and great religious figures, from every spiritual tradition or sect. The fifth Dalai Lama, for example, whilst perfectly maintaining the obligations of his elevated religious and political position, was a great practitioner of Dzogchen.

A person who is really interested in the teachings has to understand their fundamental principle without letting him or herself become conditioned by the limits of a tradition. The organizations, institutions, and hierarchies that exist in the various schools often become factors that condition us, but this is something that it is difficult for us to notice. The true value of the teachings is beyond all the superstructures people create, and to discover if the teachings are really a living thing for us we just need to observe to what extent we have freed ourselves from all the factors that condition us. Sometimes we might believe we have understood the teachings, and that we know how to apply them, but in practice we still remain conditioned by attitudes and doctrinal principles that are far from true knowledge of our own actual condition.

When a master teaches Dzogchen, he or she is trying to transmit a state of knowledge. The aim of the master is to awaken the student, opening that individual's consciousness to the primordial state. The master will not say, "Follow my rules and obey my precepts!" He will say, "Open your inner eye and observe yourself. Stop seeking an external lamp to enlighten you from outside, but light your own inner lamp. Thus the teachings will come to live in you, and you in the teachings."

The teachings must become a living knowledge in all one's daily activities. This is the essence of the practice, and besides that there is nothing in particular to be done. A monk, without giving up his vows, can perfectly well practice Dzogchen, as can a Catholic priest, a clerk, a workman, and so on, without having to abandon their role in society, because Dzogchen does not change people from the outside. Rather it awakens them internally. The only thing a Dzogchen master will ask is that one observes oneself, to gain the awareness needed to apply the teachings in everyday life.

Every religion, every spiritual teaching, has its basic philosophical principles, its characteristic way of seeing things. Within the philosophy of Buddhism alone, for example, there have arisen different systems and traditions, often disagreeing with each other only over subtleties of interpretation of the fundamental principles. In Tibet these philosophical controversies have lasted up until the present day, and the resulting polemical writings now form a whole body of literature in itself. But in Dzogchen no importance at all is attached to philosophical opinions and convictions. The way of seeing in Dzogchen is not based on intellectual knowledge, but on an awareness of the individual's own true condition.

Everyone usually has their own way of thinking and their own convictions about life, even if they can't always define them philosophically. All the philosophical theories that exist have been created by the mistaken dualistic minds of human beings. In the realm of philosophy, that which today is considered true, may tomorrow be proved to be false. No one can guarantee a philosophy's validity. Because of this, any intellectual way of seeing whatever is always partial and relative. The fact is that there is no truth to seek or to confirm logically; rather what one needs to do is to discover just how much the mind continually limits itself in a condition of dualism.

Dualism is the real root of our suffering and of all our conflicts. All our concepts and beliefs, no matter how profound they may seem, are like nets which trap us in dualism. When we discover our limits we have to try to overcome them, untying ourselves from whatever type of religious, political, or social conviction may condition us. We have to abandon such concepts as "enlightenment," "the nature of the mind," and so on, until we are no longer satisfied by a merely intellectual knowledge, and until we no longer neglect to integrate our knowledge with our actual existence.

It is therefore necessary to begin with what we know, with our human material condition. In the teaching it is explained that the individual is made up of three aspects: body, voice, and mind. These constitute our relative condition, which is subject to time and the division of subject from object. That which is beyond time and the limits of dualism is called the "absolute condition," the true state of the body, voice, and mind. To enter into this in experience, however, it is first necessary to understand our relative existence.

The body is something real for us; it is the material form which limits us within the human realm. Externally it finds its reflection in our whole material dimension, with which it is closely linked. In tantrism, for example, one speaks of precise correspondences between the human body and the universe, based on the principle of there being only one single energy. When we think of ourselves the first thing we think of is our body and our physical being. From this arises the sense of an *I*, our attachment, and all the concepts of ownership which follow from this, such as, *my* house, *my* country, *my* planet, and so on.

Through the material dimension of the body we can understand its energy, or the "voice," the second aspect of the individual. Energy is not material, visible, or tangible. It is something more subtle and difficult to understand. One of its perceivable aspects is vibration, or sound, and therefore it is known as the "voice." The voice is linked to breathing, and breathing to the individual's vital energy. In Yantra Yoga,[4] movements of the body and breathing exercises have as their aim the control of this vital energy.

The relationship between voice, breathing, and *mantra* can best be demonstrated through the way mantra functions. A mantra is a series of syllables whose power resides in its sound, through the repeated pronouncing of which one can obtain control of a given form of energy. The energy of the individual is closely linked to the external energy, and each can influence the other. Knowledge of the various aspects of the relationships between the two energies is the basis of the Bon ritual traditions, which until now have been rather overlooked by Western scholars. In Bon, for example, it is considered that many disturbances and illnesses derive from classes of beings who have the capacity to dominate certain forms of energy. When an individual's energy becomes weakened, it's like leaving a door open through which disturbances from such classes of beings can pass. Thus great importance is given to maintaining the completeness of the individual's energy.

Working from the other way round, it is possible to influence the external energy, carrying out what are called "miracles." Such activity is actually the result of having control of one's own energy, through which one obtains the capacity of power over external phenomena.

The mind is the most subtle and hidden aspect of our relative condition, but it is not difficult to notice its existence. All one has to do is to observe one's thoughts and how we let ourselves get caught up in their flow. If one asks, "What is the mind?"—the reply might be that it is the mind that asks that question. The mind is the uninterrupted flow of thoughts which arise and then disappear. It has the capacity to judge, to reason, to imagine, and so on, within the limits of space and time. But beyond the mind, beyond our thoughts, there is something we call the "nature of the mind," the mind's true condition, which is beyond all limits. If it is beyond the mind, though, how can we approach an understanding of it?

Let's take the example of a mirror. When we look into a mirror we see in it the reflected images of any objects that are in front of it; we don't see the nature of the mirror. But what do we mean by this "nature of the mirror"? We mean its capacity to reflect, definable as its clarity, its purity, and its limpidity, which are indispensable conditions for the manifestation of reflections. This "nature of the mirror" is not something visible, and the only way we can conceive of it is through the images reflected in the mirror. In the same way, we only know and have concrete experience of that which is relative to our condition of body, voice, and mind. But this itself is the way to understand their true nature.

Truly speaking, from the absolute point of view, there really does not exist any separation between the relative condition and its true nature, in the same way that a mirror and the reflections in it are in fact one indivisible whole. However, our situation is such that it is as if we have come out of the mirror and are now looking at the reflections that are appearing in it. Unaware of our own nature of clarity, purity, and limpidity, we consider the reflections to be real, developing aversion and attachment. Thus, instead of these

Refuge field

reflections being the means for us to discover our own true nature, they become a factor that conditions us. And we live distracted by the relative condition, attaching great importance to everything.

This dualistic condition, which is the general situation of all human beings, is called "ignorance" in the teachings. And even a person who has studied the most profound concepts relating to the "nature of the mind," but who does not really understand his or her relative condition, can be defined as "ignorant," because the "nature of the mind" for that person just remains an intellectual knowledge. Understanding our real nature does not necessarily require the use of the mental process of analysis and reasoning. A person who has an intellectual knowledge of the nature of the mind will remain attracted, just like any other person, by the reflections which appear and will judge them as beautiful or ugly, allowing themselves to become caught up in the mind's dualism.

In the Dzogchen teachings the term "knowledge" or the "state of knowledge" denotes a state of consciousness which is like a mirror, in that its nature cannot be stained by whatever images are reflected in it. When we find ourselves in the knowledge of our true nature, nothing can condition us. All that arises is then experienced as part of the inherent qualities of our own primordial state. For this reason the fundamental point is not to abandon or transform the relative condition, but to understand its true nature. To this end it is necessary to clear away all the misconceptions and falsifications which we continually apply to ourselves.

We have a material body, which is extremely delicate, and which has many needs we have to respect. If we are hungry we need to eat, if we are tired we need to rest, and so on. If we don't, we can develop serious health problems, because the limits of our bodies are real for us. In the teachings, overcoming attachment to the body is something spoken of a great deal. But this does not mean one should abruptly break all its limits and deny its needs. The first step to overcoming this attachment is understanding the condition of the body, and thus knowing how to respect it. This is also true with regard to the functioning of our energy. When one is ignorant of it and tries to struggle with its natural limits, the resulting disturbances can easily spread to the areas of body or mind. In Tibetan medicine, for example, some forms of madness are considered to be caused by the circulation of one of the vital subtle energies in places other than where it usually should flow.

Problems of the energy are very serious. In modern times we are living through a period in which there is an ever greater spread of illnesses, such as cancer, which are linked to disorders of the energy. The official forms of Western medicine, even if they have identified the symptoms of such illnesses, don't know what their fundamental cause is, because they don't understand how energy functions. In Tibetan medicine these types of disturbances, as and when a course of medical treatment proves ineffective, are cured through the practice of mantra, which can influence and coordinate the condition of the patient's energy through sound and breathing. Besides this, in Yantra Yoga, there are body positions, methods of controlling the breathing, and mental concentrations which can be used to restabilize disorders of the energy.

The Dzogchen teachings advise one never to force the condition of one's energy, but always to be aware of its limits in all the various circumstances one encounters. If at times one does not feel like sitting down to practice then one should avoid setting up a struggle against oneself. It could be that there is some problem of our energy that we don't know about behind our feeling like this. In such situations it is important to know how to relax, and how to give one-self space, in order not to block the progress of one's practice. Problems of loneliness, of depression, of mental confusion and so on, also often derive from an unbalanced condition of our energy.

The mind influences the condition of both the body and the energy, and at the same time depends on them. Sometimes the mind is totally enslaved by the energy and there is no way to balance it without clearing up the disorders of the energy first. It is very important to understand the relationship of interdependence between mind and energy. In all Buddhist traditions, when one is taught to meditate, it is explained that the breathing must be slow and deep, in order to favour the development of a calm state of mind. On the other hand, if we observe a nervous person whose mind is in an agitated state, we will notice right away that his or her breathing is rapid and hurried. Sometimes it is impossible to calm the mind through meditation alone, and it is necessary to practice Yantra Yoga movements and breathings in order to re-coordinate one's energy.

The image of a cage is often used as an example to represent our relative condition. An individual is said to be like a little bird closed up in and protected by a cage. The cage here is a symbol of all the limits of our body, voice, and mind. But the cage in the example is not meant to indicate some especially horrible abnormal situation; rather it is meant to describe the normal condition in which a human being lives. The problem is that we are not aware of the situation we actually find ourselves in, and are in fact afraid to discover it, because we have grown up in this cage since we were little children.

Let's consider the way a child enters into these limits. During the first months of life, when the child doesn't yet know how to reason or speak, its happy parents cradle it in their arms and whisper sweet words to it. But when the child begins to walk and wants to touch something they say, "Don't touch that! Don't go there!" Then as the child grows, it is obliged to limit more and more its way of expressing itself, its way of sitting at table, its way of eating, and so on, until it becomes a model child. The parents are then proud of it, but the truth is that the poor little thing is being made to enter completely into their way of thinking. It, too, is learning to live in a cage. And then, at five or six years of age, it begins to go to school, with all the resulting rules and expectations. The child will have a few difficulties to overcome, but it will gradually get used to this additional cage. Nowadays it takes many years to complete the cage that is indispensable to us to enable us to live in society. Then there are many further factors of conditioning, such as political ideas, religious beliefs, the ties of friendship, of work, and so on. When the cage is sufficiently developed we are ready to live in it, and we feel protected. This is the condition of every individual, and we have to discover it by observing ourselves.

When we are aware of our limits there is the possibility of overcoming them. A bird which lives in a cage gives birth to its children in the cage. When they are born, the little birds have wings. Even if, in the cage, they can't fly, the fact that they are born with wings shows that their real nature is to have contact with the open space of the sky. But if a bird that has always lived in a cage suddenly escapes from behind its bars, it could encounter many dangers, because it doesn't know what to expect out there. It may be devoured by a hawk, or caught by a cat. So it is necessary for the bird to train a little, flying about a bit in a limited space, until, when it feels ready, it can definitively take flight.

It's the same for us: even if it is difficult for us to overcome all our limits in an instant, it is important to know that our real state is there, beyond all conditioning factors, and that we really do have the possibility to rediscover it.

We can learn to fly beyond the limits of our dualistic condition, until we are ready to leave it behind altogether. We can begin by becoming aware of our body, voice, and mind. Understanding our true nature means understanding the relative condition and knowing how to reintegrate with its essential nature, so that we become once again like a mirror that can reflect any object whatsoever, manifesting its clarity.

Chapter Two
THE PATHS OF RENUNCIATION AND OF TRANSFORMATION

All the various types of teachings and spiritual paths are related to the different capacities of understanding that different individuals have. There does not exist, from an absolute point of view, any teaching which is more perfect or effective than another. A teaching's value lies solely in the inner awakening which an individual can arrive at through it. If a person benefits from a given teaching, for that person that teaching is the supreme path, because it is suited to his or her nature and capacities. There's no sense in trying to judge it as more or less elevated in relation to other paths to realization.

There are three principal paths or methods of teaching: the path of renunciation, the path of transformation, and the path of self-liberation, based, respectively, on the teachings of the Sutras, the Tantras, and on Dzogchen. These correspond to the three aspects of body, voice, and mind, called "the three gates," because they are the three ways to enter into the state of knowledge. The path of renunciation is included in the Sutra teachings, that is, in the discourses said to have been given by Buddha Shakyamuni himself. The basis of the Sutra teachings is the explanation of the Four Noble Truths: the truths of suffering, of the cause of suffering, of the cessation of suffering, and of the path that leads to this cessation. It is related that when the Buddha had reached enlightenment and met his first disciples at Sarnath, he began to transmit his knowledge to them by speaking about the experience which is most concrete and real to all beings: suffering. We are all subject to infinite types of suffering, in addition to the natural suffering of birth, sickness, old age, and death. What is the fundamental cause of all our suffering? Attachment, desire, and the passions; this is the second truth. The passions, producing karma, bind all beings into transmigration without any apparent way out. But the third truth affirms that once one has discovered the cause of transmigration, it is possible to eliminate it, extinguishing one's karma. How can this be done? By applying the path of renunciation, the fourth noble truth.

The basic principle of this "renunciation" is that, to bring about the cessation of the causes of suffering and of transmigration, it is necessary to renounce or abstain from carrying out actions that produce negative karma. At this point it is necessary to have a proper understanding of the concept of karma, because sometimes people interpret it in an imprecise or incomplete way. The fundamental idea of karma (literally, "action") is that the carrying out of a given action has given effects. These effects, however, are not irreversible. Karma is not an irrevocable law which cannot be changed. For a karma to manifest its effect appropriate conditions, known as "secondary causes" are indispensable.

When karma is explained, one generally speaks of two principal factors: primary causes and secondary causes. To produce a primary cause which is potentially capable of having an effect, three things are necessary: intention, the actual action, and then satisfaction. The primary karmic cause, formed in such a way, is comparable to the seed of a flower, whose development depends on various factors such as water, fertiliser, the sun, and so on. All these factors are like the secondary causes which make up all the different circumstances we encounter in our lives. Thus, being aware of them, it is possible to avoid favouring those which could make the primary karmic causes manifest. For example, if in a past life I have committed an action that might result in my being killed in this lifetime, this is the primary cause, which could manifest when the appropriate secondary cause, such as a quarrel, is present. But, if in the moment of quarrelling, I have the awareness that I am creating negative karma and thus refrain from becoming angry, the other person will probably calm down, and I will have avoided the possibility of being killed. In general, all secondary causes are reflections of primary causes. As the Buddha said, "If you want to know what you did in your past life, observe your present condition; if you want to know what your future condition will be, observe your present actions."

The means to fulfil the path of renunciation are through the observation of the rules of behaviour established by the Buddha, contained in the Vinaya, the code of Buddhist monastic law. By observing the precepts relating to the body, voice, and mind, it is possible to purify negative karma and accumulate positive karma. Furthermore, the maintaining of a vow is a source of merit in itself. For example, if one refrains from stealing, one accumulates a double virtue: first, for not having committed the negative action, and secondly, for maintaining the vow. This whole method is based on limiting the behaviour of the individual, principally at the level of body, that is, at the level of the material dimension.

In the Sutras, the principle of the elimination of negative karma is also the basis of the meditation practice, whose aim is that of finding a state of mental calm in which thoughts are no longer able to disturb one. By this means one avoids the possibility of producing karma through becoming caught up in one's passions. Realization is considered to be arrived at in the extinction of the individual's illusory ego, which is the root of all desires and conflicts. These concepts are, properly speaking, those of the Hinayana or Theravada Buddhist tradition, which is more faithful to the explanations given in the earliest teachings of Buddha Shakyamuni. The Mahayana, on the other hand, is based on more profound considerations, such as universal compassion and the voidness of all phenomena. In both these traditions, however, vows are a fundamental element in putting renunciation into action. When one receives monastic ordination, the external signs of renunciation of the lay world are made evident: one wears monastic robes, is given a new name, and shaves one's head. But this principle of renunciation is not only to be found exclusively in the Buddhist monastic tradition. It is also the foundation of all religious traditions and of all the nonreligious laws of society in general.

The path of transformation is to be found in the tantric teachings, the writings revealed through the pure manifestations of realized beings. To explain the fundamental principle of tantrism we can consider the symbolism of two tantric ritual objects: the *vajra* and the bell, which represent, respectively, "method," the primordial state's manifestation as form; and "energy," the "voidness" or "essence" of that which is manifest.[1] *Vajra* means "indestructible," and refers to the primordial condition of the individual, which is beyond birth and death. The bell, which represents sound, is the symbol of the energy of the primordial state. If we look at the form of the vajra, we can see that at its centre is a little sphere, from which spread out two sections, one above and one below, with five branches each. The little sphere, "thigle" (*thig le*) in Tibetan, symbolizes the primordial state's infinite potentiality to manifest, either as pure vision or *nirvana*, or as impure vision or *samsara*.

Impure vision is based on the five aggregates[2] which form the individual, and the five passions which are their functions.[3] Pure vision is the manifestation of the pure or essential aspect of the five aggregates and the five passions in the dimension of the five Buddhas of the Sambhogakaya and their corresponding wisdoms.[4] In both cases, however, the principle of the manifestation is the same: they arise from the potentiality of our primordial state. This is why the five branches of the two sections of the vajra are linked to the sphere in the centre. Samsara and nirvana are nothing other than the dualistic aspect of one single essence manifesting through energy. This energy itself is in fact inseparable from the manifestation, as is symbolized by the vajra form of the bell's handle.

The Tantras are teachings based on the knowledge and application of energy. Their origin is not to be found in the oral teachings of a master, as is the case with the Sutras taught by the Buddha, but stems from the manifestation in pure vision of a realized being. A pure manifestation arises through the energy of the elements in their subtle and luminous aspect, while our karmic vision is based on their gross or material aspect. To receive this type of transmission, it is therefore necessary to have the capacity to perceive the subtle dimension of light.

The essence of the elements is light, or colour, but this is not a matter of material colours, visible to everyone. We perceive only the colours linked to karmic vision. When these are reabsorbed into the subtle dimension of light, it is for us as if they had disappeared. But a realized being, who has purified his or her karma, and has reintegrated the material manifestation into the pure dimension of the elements, spontaneously manifests his or her wisdom through colour and light. To have contact with this pure dimension one needs to develop one's innate clarity to the highest degree, and to purify the obstacles of karma and of ignorance.

To explain the origins of the Tantras, we can take the example of one of the most well known, the Kalachakra Tantra, which is considered to have been transmitted by Buddha Shakyamuni.[5] It is clear, however, that it could not have been transmitted by the Buddha in his physical aspect, because the Kalachakra divinity is represented as being in union with his consort, a form known as "yab-yum," while the Buddha himself was a monk. This shows how the transmission of a tantra does not come about through a contact of an ordinary nature, but through the pure dimension of transformation, perceivable only by those individuals who have sufficient capacity.

What do we mean by "transformation"? We are referring to the potentiality a realized being has to manifest infinite forms in the Sambhogakaya, which forms are related to the type of beings who will perceive the transmission. At this point it is necessary to have a clear understanding of what the Sambhogakaya dimension is. *Saṃbhogakāya*, in Sanskrit, means "body" or "dimension" of wealth, the wealth being the infinite potentiality of manifestations of wisdom. This potentiality is comparable to that of a mirror at the centre of the universe which reflects all the different types of beings. Sambhogakaya manifestations are beyond time and beyond the limits of the material dimension, and their arising does not depend on there being any intention on the part of a realized being. What this means is that the manifestation of the Kalachakra divinity was not something created by the Buddha at a given moment of historical time, but is something that always existed, because the Sambhogakaya dimension is beyond time. Those who received transmission of it, through the pure perception of a manifestation of the Buddha, explained it in words and symbols, thus giving rise to the Kalachakra.

The visual representation of a manifestation of transformation is called a *mandala*, which is one of the fundamental elements of the practice of tantra. The mandala could be said to be like a photograph taken at the moment of the pure manifestation of the divinity. At the center of every mandala one finds the central divinity, who represents the primordial condition of existence, corresponding to the element of space. At the four cardinal points, represented by the colours of the other four elements, there will be the same number of forms of divinities, symbolizing the functions of wisdom which arise as the four actions.[6]

The divinity of a mandala will not always have a human appearance, but sometimes will have one or more animal heads and a corresponding number of arms and legs. This has been interpreted by many scholars as a symbolic way of representing the principles of the tantra in question. But such considerations are, in fact, only of relative and partial importance. The truth is that all manifestations of divinities arise from the Sambhogakaya dimension and since, as we have already explained, the Sambhogakaya is like a mirror, it reflects every type of being that appears to it. Thus, the so-called "Art of Tibetan Tantra" could really be seen as a kind of evidence that there do exist different types of beings all over the universe.

Let's take as an example the iconographic representation of the *dakini* Singhamukha, who has a lion's head on a woman's body. The dakinis, are, in general, a class of beings with a feminine appearance, who are manifestations of energy. Singhamukha is a Sambhogakaya form of dakini. Her name, in Sanskrit, means "lion faced," because her face is similar to a lion's, in particular to that of the mythical snow lion of Tibet. For the lack of any other way to say what she is like, the convention arose that this dakini has a lion's face. But one cannot exclude the possibility that what is really represented is a type of being we don't know about.

Another example of this kind of thing is the wrathful divinity Yamantaka, who is represented as having the head of a buffalo. He is considered to be the Sambhogakaya manifestation of the Bodhisattva Manjushri, a manifestation received by a class of beings called the "Yama," whose particular characteristic is in fact that of having a head similar to a buffalo's.

The manifestation of the Sambhogakaya comes about through three factors: sound, light, and rays. Sound is the first stage of the manifestation of energy, which, in the dimension of manifestation, is perceived as mantra. This type of mantra, called the "Natural Sound of the Vajra" since it arises spontaneously, is used in practice to integrate the visualization (of the mandala of the divinity) with the function of one's own energy. Light, the second stage of manifestation, is the visible aspect of energy, energy still in a phase prior to its assuming any specific form. And then, thirdly, through the rays manifest all the infinite forms and colours of the mandala of the divinity. Every individual potentially possesses these three aspects of manifestation.

There is a tantric saying which goes, "One applies the fruit like the path," because the dimension of the mandala— a manifestation of realization or the *fruit* —becomes the path for the disciple's realization through the oral and symbolic transmission given by a master. Many texts state that various tantras were originally transmitted to Indian *mahasiddhas* who were going to the country of Oddiyana and who, while still on the way there, received transmission by means of visions. Oddiyana, which was the original source of both the Tantras and Dzogchen, and was the native country of masters such as Garab Dorje and Padmasambhava, is sometimes called "The Land of the Dakinis," a phrase used to indicate the concentration, in a specific place, of these manifestations of the energy of the universe.

The realized masters who "imported" the Tantras into the human world from various dimensions, transmitted the pure dimension of transformation through representations of the mandala. This transmission takes place every time a master confers the initiation of a tantra on a disciple.

During the initiation the master describes the image of the mandala to be visualized, and in particular the divinity into which one has to transform oneself. Then, himself visualizing the dimension of the transformation, he confers the empowerment for the practice, transmitting the natural sound of the mantra specific to the divinity. After the disciple has received the initiation and has thus had his or her first experience of transformation into pure vision, he or she is then ready to apply this as the path, through visualization and through the recitation of mantra. By these means the practitioner of Tantra tries to transform ordinary impure vision into the pure vision of the mandala of the divinity. All tantras are based on the principle of transformation, working with the knowledge of how energy functions. The very meaning of the word *tantra*—"continuation"—refers to the nature of the energy of the primordial state, which manifests without interruption.

The practice of tantra has two phases: the development stage (*bskyed rim*), and the "perfectioning" stage (*rdzogs rim*). The first phase consists of the gradual visualization of the mandala, beginning with the seed syllable of the principal divinity, and the syllables of the four elements. When the imaginary creation of the mandala is complete, whilst maintaining the visualization of oneself transformed into the form of the central divinity, one recites the mantra. In this phase one works a great deal with the imaginative faculty of the mind, trying to develop to the maximum one's capacity to visualize. The second phase, the "perfectioning" stage, focuses on the visualization of the internal mandala of the *chakra* and the *nadi*,[7] and on concentration on the syllables of the mantra, which turns without interruption around the central seed syllable. At the end of the session of practice, both the external and the internal mandalas are integrated into the dimension of the body, voice, and mind of the practitioner. The final result of the practice is that pure vision manifests without depending any longer on the visualization, becoming part of one's natural clarity. Thus, one realizes the total state of reintegration of pure vision with impure vision, the *Mahamudra*, the "great symbol" in which samsara and nirvana are indissolubly united.

This method of practice, based on gradual transformation, is to be found in the Mahayoga tradition of the Nyingmapa school and in the Anuttara Tantra tradition of all the other schools.[8] But there also exists a Tantric method based on instantaneous, nongradual visualization, which is found only in the Anuyoga tradition. The principle of this Anuyoga method is that since, in the primordial state of every individual, the mandala and the divinity are self perfected from the very beginning, elaborate gradual visualizations are not necessary. Therefore, all that is required in this method is the immediate presence of the dimension of the mandala, manifested in an instant. Furthermore, this practice is principally based on the perfectioning stage of visualization. In the Anuyoga, the state of total reintegration that results from successful practice is not called Mahamudra, but "Dzogchen." This shows that the principle of self-perfectedness that is the basis of this method is the same as that in the Dzogchen teachings, although the actual path is different.

When one has really and truly obtained the capacity of transformation, one can activate it in one's daily behaviour through transforming the passions into wisdoms. Three principal passions are spoken of in Buddhism: anger, attachment, and mental obscuration—called the "three poisons" because they are the cause of transmigration. In tantrism it is considered that these poisons can be transformed into wisdom through three specific methods of transformation: through transforming oneself into the wrathful form of the divinity to overcome anger, into the joyous form to overcome attachment, and into the peaceful form to overcome mental obscuration.[9] Training in the practice of transformation with these forms of the divinity, the practitioner is able to succeed in overcoming the passions, transforming them into their corresponding wisdoms.

Let's take a concrete example of this type of practice. Suppose one becomes angry with someone and experiences a strong sensation of anger; what one does is to try, in that very instant, to visualize oneself transformed into the wrathful form of the divinity, in the pure dimension of the Sambhogakaya. In this manner the anger can be increased to the point where it causes the very universe itself to tremble, but since there no longer remains for the practitioner any dualistic division of reality into subject and object, the anger liberates itself as pure energy, without any target to be directed against.

In the same circumstances a practitioner of the path of renunciation would try to "block" the anger, thinking of the consequences of the negative karma. So we can easily understand the difference between the various methods used in these practices. The practitioner of the path of renunciation, even if he or she really "feels" anger arise in him or herself, tries at all costs to avoid it, as if afraid of facing it. In a certain sense, such a practitioner can be said to be ignorant of the nature of energy. The tantric practitioner, however, is aware of how energy functions, and knows that blocking energy can cause disturbances to the body as well as to the mind. He or she does not put the brakes on the flow of energy, does not repress it, but uses it as a means for transformation. To do this, however, requires a highly developed capacity of practice.

In general terms, these are the characteristics of the paths of Sutra and Tantra. In Dzogchen, on the other hand, the method of self-liberation is taught right away, a method in which there is nothing to renounce or to transform. If one does not have sufficient capacity, however, this self-liberation will not bring real results. For this reason, in the Dzogchen teachings it is advised that one should know how to apply whatever kind of method is most adapted to the circumstances one finds oneself in, and most suited to one's level of capacity, until one has really acquired knowledge of the state of self-liberation. This is something the practitioner him or herself must be aware of.

Chapter Three
THE PATH OF SELF-LIBERATION

The Dzogchen teachings are also known as Atiyoga, or "primordial yoga." The word *yoga* is used here with the sense that it has in the equivalent Tibetan term *naljor* (*rnal 'byor*), which means "possessing the authentic condition," this condition being the primordial state of each individual. A further name for Dzogchen is "the teaching of the state of mind of Samantabhadra," or primordial enlightenment.[1] The method practiced in the path of Dzogchen is called "self-liberation" because it is based on knowledge and understanding. But it is not that there is some object that has to be known; rather it is a matter of entering into the experience of a state beyond the reasoning mind, the state of contemplation. There is no way to begin to understand this state however, if one does not take the mind as one's starting point. That is why the path of self-liberation is said to be more linked to the factor of mind than the paths of renunciation and transformation. In Dzogchen, introduction is given directly to the inherent state of the individual, by means of an explanation of the primordial base of existence which is the original condition of all beings.

In both the Sutras and the Tantras one of the fundamental concepts discussed is that of the "nature of the mind," the true condition of the mind, which is beyond the limits of the intellect and of time. The basic principle here is that of voidness or *shunyata*, the central doctrine of the Mahayana. The meaning of the term *voidness* as it is used in the *Prajñaparamita*,[2] is the absence of substantiality—or of self-nature—of all phenomena, which is the real, inherent condition of all existence.[3] When referring to the individual, this condition is referred to as the "nature of the mind."

In the Dzogchen teachings many terms are used to denote the nature of the mind, including, the "primordial base" (*ye gzhi*); the "base of everything" (*kun gzhi*); the "essence of primordial *bodhichitta*" (*ye gzhi snying po byang chub kyi sems*), and so on. This last term is found in many ancient Dzogchen texts, and it will be useful to explain its meaning.

In the Mahayana, bodhichitta is taken as meaning the commitment, based on a feeling of universal compassion, to bringing all beings to enlightenment. Two types of bodhichitta are spoken of in particular: relative and absolute. The relative bodhichitta consists of the training of one's thoughts to develop the intention to benefit others and the actual carrying out of altruistic actions. The absolute bodhichitta is the knowledge of the voidness of all phenomena, and comes close to the concept of "primordial bodhichitta" in Dzogchen.

When translated into Tibetan, *bodhichitta* becomes "chang chub sem" (*byang chub sems*), a term made up of three words: "chang" (*byang*), which means "purified"; "chub," meaning "perfected"; and "sem" (*sems*), which means "mind." "Mind" stands for the "nature of the mind"; "purified" means that all obstacles and negativities have been purified; and "perfected" means that all the attainments and qualities have been realized. So the primordial bodhichitta is the state of the individual, which is from the very beginning without obstacles, perfect, and includes as its potentiality all the various manifestations of energy. It is a condition which is beyond time, beyond dualism, pure and perfect like the nature of the mirror. If one is ignorant of it, however, it is not manifest and it becomes necessary to remove the provisional obstacles that obscure it.

In the Dzogchen teachings the primordial state of the *base* is not defined only as being void, but is explained as having three aspects or characteristics, called the "three primordial wisdoms": *essence, nature,* and *energy.*

The *essence* is the void, the real condition of the individual and of all phenomena. This base is the condition of all individuals, whether they are aware of it or not, whether they are enlightened or in transmigration. It is said to be "pure from the beginning" (*ka dag*), because, like space, it is free of all impediments, and is the basis of all the manifestations in existence.

The manifestation of the primordial state in all its aspects, its "clarity," on the other hand, is called the *nature.* It is said to be "self-perfected" (*lhun grub*), because it exists spontaneously from the beginning, like the sun which shines in space. *Clarity* is the pure quality of all thought and of all perceived phenomena, uncontaminated by mental judgment. For example, when we see a flower, we first perceive its image without the mind entering into judgment, even if this phase of perception only lasts for a fraction of a second. Then, in a second phase, mental judgment enters into the situation and one categorizes the perception, thinking, "That's a flower, it's red, it has a specific scent, and so on." Developing from this, attachment and aversion, acceptance and rejection all arise, with the consequent creation of karma and transmigration. Clarity is the phase in which perception is vivid and present, but the mind has not yet entered into action. It is the spontaneous manifestation of the individual's state. The same is true for thoughts: if we don't follow them, and don't become caught up in mental judgment, they too are part of our natural clarity.

The third of the three primordial wisdoms is *energy*. Its characteristic is that it manifests without interruption.[4] The explanation of energy in Dzogchen is fundamental to understanding the base. All dimensions, whether pure or impure, material or subtle, are manifestations of one aspect or another of energy. To explain how both transmigration and enlightenment originate, three ways in which energy manifests are described. These three modes of energy are called "tsel" (*rtsal*), "rolba" (*rol ba*) , and "dang" (*gdangs*), names that cannot be translated into Western languages.

To understand the manifestation of energy as *tsel*, we can take the example of what happens when a crystal ball is placed near a window. The crystal is pure and transparent, but when rays of light strike it, they refract into coloured lights all around the room. These lights are not inherent to the crystal itself, but manifest when the appropriate secondary cause is present, in this case the sun's rays. The crystal ball symbolizes the primordial state of the individual, which consists of essence, nature, and energy. The coloured rays which spread in the room are an example of the natural manifestation of energy, appearing in relation to the individual as an object. In the moment of the manifestation of the energy of the primordial state, if one recognizes it as a projection of one's own original qualities, one realizes oneself in the dimension of pure vision. If the opposite happens and one perceives the rays and colours as being external to oneself, one manifests impure vision. Thus the cause of both visions, samsara and nirvana, is the same: the manifestation of the light of the primordial state.

As an example of *rolba*, we should imagine that instead of the colours reflecting externally to the crystal, this time they reflect inside it, not appearing outside the crystal but within its own surfaces. In the same way, the energy of the primordial state can manifest within its own dimension "subjectively" in relation to the individual. This happens, for example, in the *bardo*, the intermediate state between death and rebirth, when the hundred peaceful and wrathful divinities appear. They are not external to the individual, but are the manifestations of his or her natural, self-perfected qualities. The appearance of these divinities, however, only arises for those who have, in their lifetime, received transmission from a master, and applied the method of transformation specific to the peaceful and wrathful divinities. For an ordinary being there arises only the manifestation of "sounds, rays, and lights," which may last only for an instant, and most often are a cause of alarm.[5] For this reason, great importance is given in tantrism to knowledge of the mode of energy of *rolba*, which is the basis of all the various methods of transformation.

To understand *dang* we should think of the crystal itself, and of its pure and transparent form. If we put a crystal ball at the centre of a coloured mandala and walk around it, the crystal will by turns appear to assume the colours of the cardinal points of the mandala at which we successively arrive, while at the same time remaining, in itself, pure and transparent. This is an example of the inherent condition of energy itself as it really is, in any kind of manifestation whatsoever. Sometimes instead of *dang* the term "gyen" *(rgyan)* is used, meaning "ornament," because in the state of contemplation all manifestations of energy are "perceived" as ornaments of the primordial state.

When the introduction has been given by the master, the essence, nature, and energy are called the "three bodies of the base." They correspond, in the path, to three aspects or

characteristic conditions of the nature of the mind: the calm
state (*gnas pa*), movement (*'gyu ba*) and presence (*rig pa*).

The calm state is the condition of the mind in which no
thoughts arise. An example of this is the space that exists
between the disappearing of one thought and the arising of
another, a space that is usually imperceptible. The movement is the manifestation of thoughts, without interruption.
An example is given in which the state without thoughts is
said to be like a calm lake, and the arising of thoughts to be
like the movement of fish in the lake. These two factors are
common to all beings. Presence,[6] on the other hand, is as if
asleep in us, and it takes a master to awaken it through transmission. Presence is the pure recognition without judgment,
of either the calm state or the movement. These three are
called the "three bodies of the path."

In the *fruit*, or realization, they manifest as Dharmakaya,
Sambhogakaya, and Nirmanakaya, the three "purified dimensions." The Dharmakaya corresponds to the condition
of the essence, the voidness of all phenomena. However,
presence is here totally awakened. The state of the
Dharmakaya is beyond form or colour, like limitless space.
The Sambhogakaya is the self-perfected dimension of the
manifestation of energy. It corresponds to the natural clarity of the base, linked to presence. The Nirmanakaya is the
dimension of manifestation whether pure or impure, perceived as an object in relation to one's own state, although
there no longer remains any trace of dualism. Presence is
totally integrated with the external dimension.[7]

No matter how many analyses one does, one should not
forget that one is always referring to one's own condition,
to the aspects of one's own body, voice, and mind. If one
tries to understand a teaching with this attitude, whatever
explanation one receives will be meaningful, and will not
remain something abstract. I remember when I was a boy in

Garab Dorje, showing with his right hand
the mudra of "Direct Introduction"

Tibet, I studied in depth a commentary on the *Prajñaparamita-sutra*, the *Abhisamayalankara*,[8] and became expert in expounding on its content. But I didn't succeed in understanding its real meaning, because all the descriptions it contained of the different levels of the buddhas and bodhisattvas seemed to me to be totally apart from my own condition. My college teacher probably noticed this, because one day he said to me, "When you read these descriptions of the buddhas and so on, you should understand that they are descriptions of your own condition." I tried to put his advice into practice, but I found it extremely difficult. It was only some years later, when I came to have knowledge of Dzogchen, that I understood the meaning of my college master's words. Then, when I reread that text, it was as if I was reading it for the first time, and it had a whole new meaning for me.

The practice of Dzogchen is based on two fundamental aspects of the nature of the individual: the calm state, and the movement of thought through which it is necessary for one to find oneself integrated in the state of presence. In some Buddhist traditions much importance is given to meditation in order to find oneself in a calm state, known as "shinay" (*zhi gnas*), the goal of which is to relax the mind into a condition without thoughts, or not disturbed by their movement. Sometimes, however, there is the danger that one will become sleepy in such states, and thus block the progress of the practice. For this reason it is considered important in the Dzogchen teachings to know how to work with the energy of this movement itself, which is an inherent aspect of the individual.

In tantrism, too, practice is based on working with movement, but in this case, on an imaginary movement, created by the mind. The goal here, however, is not to find a peaceful state without thought. Rather, through working with one's imagination, one creates the pure dimension of the mandala, beginning with the elements of air, water, fire, and so on. This activity is movement. But until one realizes the Mahamudra, one cannot easily succeed in integrating one's own energy with the ordinary movement of the material dimension.

In Dzogchen, too, various methods of using energy are practiced, but these are not based on the activity of the mind. Their principle is direct integration of the manifestations of energy with the state of presence. It makes no difference whether there appears before one's mind the pure vision of a mandala, or there appears before one's eyes the karmic vision of a room: both are regarded as part of one's clarity. Whether one finds oneself in a calm state, or in a pure manifestation of movement, these are both experiences and are not the state of contemplation itself. In the state of presence, which remains the same in relation to thousands of different experiences, whatever arises liberates itself automatically. This is what is meant by "self-liberation."

This self-liberation is exactly what has to be applied in one's conduct in daily life. Taking the example of the passion of anger, we have described the different ways in which a practitioner of the path of renunciation and a practitioner of the path of transformation will react. We have also said that the transformation of the passions into wisdoms, which is the method of the Tantras, requires a higher level of capacity, which is the result of many years of training. In the concept of transformation, however, there still remains a sense of dualism. That is to say, there is on the one hand a passion, and on the other its transformation into wisdom.

But a practitioner of Dzogchen, in the moment of becoming angry, attempts neither to block nor to transform the passion, but observes it without judging it. In this way the anger will dissolve by itself, as if it had been left in its natural condition, allowing it to liberate of itself.

In general, when a thought or a passion arises, one can distinguish two distinct phases. In the first there arises the movement, of anger, for example, and in the second one lets oneself get involved in mental judgment and enters into action. To apply the method of self-liberation it is important to observe the moment in which the mind has not yet entered into judgment. When one maintains the state of presence, any thought or movement whatever can be compared to a cloud as big as an egg, which gets bigger little by little until it becomes as big as a mountain, and finally, in the same way that it arose, gets smaller and smaller again until it disappears altogether.

Knowledge of the state of self-liberation is the foundation of the practice of Dzogchen. It is said that "the practitioner of Dzogchen meditates without meditating," which seems to be just a play on words, but is really true. The most important thing is never to become distracted, maintaining the state of presence in every moment.

There is a story that tells how a learned monk went to visit Yunton (gYung ston),[9] a Dzogchen master who lived simply, surrounded by a large number of disciples. The monk, who had studied Buddhist doctrines for years, and felt himself to be learned, in the grip of jealousy thought, "How does he, an ordinary person, dare to teach? How dare he pretend to be a master if he doesn't even wear monk's robes? I will go and confront his knowledge with mine, and humiliate him in front of his disciples, so that they will leave him and follow me." Full of pride and arrogance he went to Yunton and asked him, "You practitioners of Dzogchen, are you always meditating?" To which Yunton replied, "What is there to meditate on?"

"So," the monk continued, "you don't meditate then?" Yunton replied, "When am I ever distracted?"

Chapter Four
THE IMPORTANCE OF TRANSMISSION

The Dzogchen teachings are linked to a transmission, which resides in the master, and which is of fundamental importance for the development of the knowledge and realization of the disciples. In the Sutras it is taught that enlightenment is only possible after many lifetimes dedicated to practice; in the Tantras on the other hand, it is said that one can reach enlightenment in one single lifetime, because the methods used are much more effective. In Dzogchen, however, realization is not only considered to be attainable in one lifetime, but the "Great Transference into the Body of Light" is also spoken of. This particular realization, which was actually accomplished by masters such as Padmasambhava and Vimalamitra, and by Tapihritsa[1] in the Bon tradition, involves the transference or reabsorption, without a physical death, of the material body into the luminous essence of the elements, in the course of which realization the physical body disappears from the sight of ordinary beings. If one does not succeed in realizing this Body of Light in one's lifetime, one can realize it after one's death, as has happened to many practitioners of Dzogchen in Tibet in recent times. This realization depends not only on the specific methods found in Dzogchen,[2] but also primarily on the function of the transmission from the master.

When a Dzogchen master teaches, he or she transmits the state of knowledge through three types of transmission: oral, symbolic, and direct. In Dzogchen, rituals of initiation are not indispensable, as they are in tantrism. The real meaning of initiation is transmission of the state of knowledge, and this can take place through just the giving of a simple explanation. Everything depends on the disciple's capacity to understand.

Some masters of the Nyingmapa tradition have taught that the three transmissions refer to the origins of the Dzogchen teachings. They say that Dzogchen was first transmitted by Samantabhadra (the Dharmakaya) to Vajrasattva[3] (the Sambhogakaya), and that then, from them, it was transmitted to Garab Dorje (the Nirmanakaya), by means of symbolic transmission. From Garab Dorje, through oral transmission, it was then received by human beings. This explanation makes it seem as if there were three different masters who gave three different kinds of teachings. But in fact the three transmissions are all inseparable from the master, and they themselves are the "path." If direct transmission had come from the Dharmakaya to the Sambhogakaya it could not be a path, because the Sambhogakaya has no need of a path. The individual is, in fact, made up of body, voice, and mind all at the same time, and so it is that all three types of transmission are used by the master to communicate the state of knowledge.

The oral transmission includes both explanations given by the master to bring the disciple to understand the nature of the primordial state, and methods of practice to enable one to enter into the knowledge of the state.

Symbolic transmission takes place both through symbolic objects, such as a mirror or a piece of crystal, which are shown to the disciple by the master in order to transmit knowledge of the primordial state, and through stories, parables, and riddles.[4]

The direct transmission comes about through the unification of the state of the master with that of the disciple. An example of direct transmission can be found in the story of the awakening of Naropa, the famous Indian *mahasiddha*, who was a disciple of Tilopa.[5] Naropa was a famous pandit, a great and learned scholar, and the abbot of Nalanda University, one of the most important centers of Buddhist culture in medieval India. Naropa's knowledge, however, remained at an intellectual doctrinaire level, and was not a lived state of knowledge.

After several years at Nalanda, following some signs and indications of a visionary nature, he renounced his responsibility as abbot and set off in search of Tilopa, who, according to his visions, would be the master capable of awakening him. After a long and exhausting search, during which he met Tilopa in various guises without recognizing him, Naropa finally bumped into a fisherman who called himself Tilopa. This latter was frying fish in a pan, and with a snap of his fingers was then bringing the fish back to life and throwing them back in the water. Naropa was profoundly disturbed by this meeting, but had faith in his master and followed him for many years, continuously serving him. Throughout this whole time he received no teachings whatsoever, but Tilopa continually put him to the test of various acts of self-denial. One day, when master and disciple were in a mountain cave, Tilopa asked Naropa to go down into the valley to get him some water to drink. Naropa, despite the sultry heat, after expending a great deal energy, managed to climb back up with some water. As soon as he saw him Tilopa took off one sandal and struck Naropa on the forehead with it. Naropa fell down, stunned. When he came to his senses once again he was greatly changed; knowledge had been awakened in him. But this was not a miracle carried out by Tilopa. For years and years Naropa had made a continual self-sacrifice, preparing himself to receive transmission.

The value of transmission is not only that of introducing the state of knowledge, but lies also in its function of bringing about the maturing of the transmission, right up until one reaches realization. For this reason the relationship that links master and disciple is a very close one. The master, in Dzogchen, is not just like a friend who helps and collaborates with the disciple; rather the master is himself or herself the path. This is because the practice of contemplation develops through the unification of the state of the disciple with that of the master. The master is extremely important, too, at the Sutra and the Tantra levels of teaching, in the former because he or she is the holder of Buddha's teachings, and in the latter because he or she is the source of all the manifestations of transformation.

To illustrate this last point, there is a story that tells that when Padmasambhava transmitted the initiation of Vajra Kilaya[6] to his Tibetan disciples, he made a mandala of that divinity miraculously appear in front of them, asking them to pay homage. The disciples got up and prostrated in front of the mandala, except for Yeshe Tsogyel.[7] She alone paid homage to Padmasambhava, because she had understood that the master is the root source of manifestations.

The master is the gateway to knowledge for the disciple, and his or her transmission is always present in a practitioner's life. One can receive teachings from various

masters, without any limits, but usually there is one particular master who causes the state of knowledge to arise in
a given individual, and this master is known as that
individual's "root master" *(rtsa ba'i bla ma)*. I myself, when I
was in Tibet, met many masters who gave me teachings and
initiations, but there was one master in particular,
Changchub Dorje (Byang chub rdo rje), who opened the door
to knowledge for me.

Two years before I met this master I had a dream. I
dreamed that I was in a place I didn't know with many
houses built of white concrete, a style of building rarely
found in Tibet, where the houses were usually built of stone
and were of colours other than white. The houses in my
dream were similar to those that the Chinese had begun to
build a few years before that time in some areas of eastern
Tibet. I went close to one of the houses and saw that there
was written above its door, in gold letters on a blue back-
ground, the mantra of Padmasambhava. I went in and saw
an old man, who seemed just like a normal country person
of Tibet. While I was still asking myself if this could possi-
bly be a master, I heard him begin to recite the mantra of
Padmasambhava. Then he said to me, "On the other side of
this mountain, within the rock face, there is a cave in which
there are eight natural mandalas; go there right away and
look at them!" Amazed, still dreaming, I at once began climb-
ing the mountain, with my father following me. When we
entered the cave my father began reciting the *Prajñaparamita-
sutra* aloud, and I joined in with him. We walked around
inside the cave looking at its walls, but I only succeeded in
seeing some ornamental details of the eight mandalas. At
this point, still reciting the sutra, I woke up.

Later, in 1956, the daughter of a noble family of my area
of Tibet became seriously ill, and despite the attempts of
several doctors to cure her, she did not get any better. Her

parents, who had heard of a master who was also a doctor with a reputation of being able to cure difficult cases, decided to send some servants to this doctor to seek a remedy for their daughter's illness. After two days' journey on horseback, the servants reached the master's place of residence, where they were welcomed and invited right away to rest. But the next day the master told them that all medicines would now be of no avail, since the sick girl had died three days after their departure. When the servants returned home, they reported everything that had happened and discovered that the girl had in fact died shortly after they had left.

One day, a little later, the girl's father, who was a friend of my family, arrived to visit my father, and told him all about the master-doctor, describing him as an old country person who lived in a village with many houses made of white cement. I was listening to his story together with my father, and I at once remembered my dream. That same evening I asked my father permission to go visit that master. After two days of preparation for the journey I set off, together with my father, and when we reached the master's village I noticed that the place was exactly as I had seen it in my dream. The master welcomed us as if he already knew us. He was a very simple person, who lived as the doctor of the village, surrounded by a small community of disciples who worked and practiced together harmoniously. The people of the village said that when the master had first arrived there he had said that he was seventy years old, and that from that moment on he always continued, year after year, to say he was the same age. Calculating the number of years that had elapsed since he came to the village, one could conclude that at the time of our visit he was 130 years old.

I remained for several months with this master. During my days there I had a certain amount of difficulty adjusting to the situation, because I was used to important masters who gave teachings and initiations in formal, traditional style. Changchub Dorje, on the other hand, seemed not to be giving me teachings at all, whereas in fact he was actually teaching me to break out of the cage I had constructed for myself. I became aware that, even after so many years of study, I had not yet understood the real meaning of the teachings. But I nevertheless did not feel satisfied, because this master had not given me any initiations. When I asked Changchub Dorje to give me an initiation however, he replied, "You don't need a ritual initiation, you've already received a lot of them from many other masters." But I answered that I wanted to receive one from him, and finally, after considerable insistence on my part, he agreed. He decided to give me the initiation of the one hundred peaceful and wrathful divinities and, since he was not expert in carrying out rituals, he had a disciple who was good at such things help him. That initiation, which usually doesn't take long to give, took him all day to complete. Changchub Dorje did not know how to carry out the various phases of the ritual, and in fact could not even read fluently. There is a part in such rituals where, to transmit the empowerment through the mantras, the one giving the initiation sounds the bell and *damaru*[8] simultaneously. But Changchub Dorje first sounded the bell, and then the damaru, and then recited the mantra. I was very surprised because I knew very well how the various phases of such ritual initiations should be carried out.

That evening, at the end of the initiation, Changchub Dorje spoke to me and made me understand the real meaning of initiation. At the end of an initiation masters usually show the disciple the text containing the ritual, and describe the lineage of masters who have transmitted it. But Changchub Dorje didn't show me a book. Rather, for three hours, without interruption, he spoke to me about the real meaning of the Dzogchen teachings. It seemed almost as if he was reciting a tantra of Dzogchen,[9] so perfect and so profound were the words he spoke. He concluded by saying, "This is the complete transmission of all the three series of the Dzogchen teachings; of the series of the Nature of the Mind, of the series of Primordial Space, and of the Series of Secret Instructions." With this he really turned all my ideas upside down, and all the limits of my intellectual knowledge collapsed. Changchub Dorje had opened a door, and had made me understand that the teachings live in the individual.

He had never received a formal scholastic education, and had never studied. His knowledge was the fruit of the internal awakening that had changed his life. He was also a revealer of *terma*, or "terton" *(gter ston)*, and I myself sometimes used to take dictation from him of some of his revelations. He usually spent his days seated in front of his house, outside an open window, receiving his patients. I would sit inside the house, at the other side of the window, and, in the intervals between one patient's visit and the next, he would dictate something to me and I would write it down. Then, when the next patient reached him, he would break off from his dictation. But when he began to dictate to me again, after that patient had left, he would continue the sentence just where he had paused in it, without even ever having to ask me at what point he had left off dictating.[10]

One of Changchub Dorje's principal masters had been Pema Dundul (Pad ma bdud 'dul),[11] who was also a very simple master, and who became famous after his death for having realized the Body of Light. Usually one who practices this realization, when he or she decides to die, asks to be left closed up inside a room or a tent for seven days. Then on the eighth day, only their hair and nails, considered to be the impurities of the body, are found.

The story goes that Pema Dundul, about twenty days before he died, called together all his principal disciples and gave to them all the teachings and transmissions that he had not previously given them. My master, Changchub Dorje, was one of his disciples, and was there. Then they practiced the *ganapuja*[12] together for many days until, on the eleventh day of the lunar calendar, a day considered to be specially linked with Padmasambhava, Pema Dundul asked them all to accompany him up the mountain to the place in which he had chosen to die. When they got there and his little tent had been set up, the master asked them to sew up its door, and to come back after a week had passed. It is said that, during those seven days, it rained heavily and many rainbows appeared. On the eighth day, when his disciples reopened the tent, they found only his clothes, still in the same position in which the master had sat when he went into the tent. His fabric belt, which tied his traditional Tibetan clothes at the waist, remained still tied around the clothes as if there was still a person inside them. Pema Dundul had been a very simple practitioner who had no fixed abode, but had wandered about all his life, practicing the Chod *(gcod)*.[13] He was the master of Ayu Khandro (A yu mkha' 'gro),[14] one of my masters, who spent more than fifty years of her life in a retreat in the dark.

In 1949 there was another example of a person realizing the Body of Light. A monk from a Sakyapa monastery, in which the rules were very strict, became involved in a relationship with a girl. When this was discovered, the people running the monastery had him beaten and driven out. Sad and without a home, this monk then went off towards northwestern Tibet where he had the good fortune to meet Tsangpa Drubchen (gTsang pa grub chen),[15] a Dzogchen master who had twelve children, all of them practitioners. They all lived as nomads, raising cattle. The monk stayed with them for almost two years, working with them and receiving many teachings. Then he decided to return to his own area, but he was not given permission to live in his old house, which was inside the monastery. So he built a small retreat house for himself on a site that enabled him to at least see the monastery. The woman with whom he had previously had the relationship went to live with him, acting as his assistant for his retreats and taking care of their cattle. Thus they lived together for several years, until one day the ex-monk announced that he would die in seven days' time. He went to the monastery officials and arranged with them that at least half his belongings should be given to his lady companion after his death. In Tibet, when a monk died all his worldly goods would usually go, by right, to the monastery. So after resolving this situation to his satisfaction, he then asked to be left undisturbed in his room for a week. At dawn on the eighth day, many monks and officials of the monastery came together to take part in the event, even though they had always criticized and mistreated this man in his lifetime. When they opened the room, only his nails and hair remained. A golden tomb was built in the monastery to contain these remains.

Still more recently, in 1952, my uncle[16] witnessed another such event. Near where I lived in Tibet, there lived an old man who earned his living by carving mantras on rocks. When he was young he had at first been a tailor, then groom to the horses belonging to a famous master called Dodrub Chen (rDo grub chen),[17] from whom he had probably received some teachings. Before he died he left all his belongings to the monastery in which his son was a monk, and announced that within a week he would be dead. Everybody was amazed, because no one considered him to be a practitioner. But when he gave instructions that he be closed up in a tent for seven days, they understood that he had realized the Body of Light. On the eighth day many people rushed to take part in what was going to happen, including some Chinese officials who were convinced that they would be able to show once and for all how foolishly superstitious the Tibetan people were. But in this case, too, when the tent was opened, all that was found inside was the practitioner's hair and nails.

I remember how my uncle, who was present at the opening of the tent, returned in tears saying, "I knew him for years and years without ever realizing that he was such a high practitioner!" But many Dzogchen practitioners are like that, simple people, who, even if they show no external sign of it, possess real knowledge. The Body of Light is the supreme realization of Dzogchen. Its function is different from that of a Sambhogakaya manifestation, because a being in a Body of Light can communicate and actively help other beings. It is as if the physical body, its material substance having been absorbed into its luminous essence, continues to live as an aggregation of the elements in their subtle aspect. Manifestations of the Sambhogakaya, on the other hand, are passive, because they depend on the beings who enjoy the vision of them.

Realization is not something one can construct, and does not depend on one's actions or effort. Becoming realized basically means just overcoming one's provisional obstacles, and to this end the transmission from one's master is of the greatest help. In Dzogchen, the path to overcoming obstacles can be very rapid because, through the transmission, one can easily develop the state of contemplation. From our limited point of view, we can get discouraged thinking that to purify our karma will take many lifetimes. If we could actually materially see our accumulated karma, the good karma might seem like a small rock, compared to a huge mountain of negative karma. How long would it take to purify all that? It might seem perhaps that even hundreds of purification practices would only diminish the mountain of our negative karma by nothing more than the length of a finger.

But karma is not in fact a material accumulation, and does not depend on externals; rather its power to condition us depends on the obstacles that impede our knowledge. If we compare our karma and the ignorance that creates it to a dark room, knowledge of the primordial state would be like a lamp, which, when lit in the room, at once causes the darkness to disappear, enlightening everything. In the same way, if one has the presence of the primordial state, one can overcome all hindrances in an instant.

A practitioner who is just beginning to try to find the state of presence among the confusion of all of his or her thoughts is like a blind person trying to push a thread through the eye of a needle. The master is like someone who sees and helps that person to get his or her hands closer to where they have to be. When the blind person succeeds in threading the needle, it is as if their sight had returned to them. This is how it is the moment one recognizes and enters into the primordial state by means of the transmission.

The example of the sky, the sun, and clouds, is given to explain the condition of the individual. The sky is not a definable place, it has no shape or colour, and no one can say where it starts or finishes. It is something universal, as is the primordial state of the individual, the void. The *base*, at the level of the individual, is like the space inside a clay vase, which, even though it is temporarily limited by the shape of the vase, is not different from the space outside, surrounding the vase. This void condition which is like empty space is called the *essence*, and it is beyond all concepts. But in it there is a continuous *clarity* that manifests in the individual's thoughts and the various aspects of *energy*; this clarity is the state of presence, which is like a sun arising in the sky.

The light of the sun is the manifestation of the clarity of the sky; and the sky is the basic condition necessary for the manifestation of the sun's light. So, too, in the sky two, three, four, or any number of suns could arise; but the sky always remains indivisibly one sky. Similarly, every individual's state of presence is unique and distinct, but the void nature of the individual is universal, and common to all beings.

Lastly, we have the example of clouds, which represent the provisional hindrances that impede the manifestation of our primordial state. When clouds grow dense, it is as if the sun did not exist, but the fact is that the sun has not changed its position at all. Both day and night, the sun is always there, but its rays don't always light up the earth. In the same way, the primordial state of knowledge is always there in the individual right from the beginning, whether one transmigrates or is enlightened, but if it does not manifest, it is because of our ignorance. Enlightenment, or nirvana, is nothing other than the state beyond all obstacles, in the same way that from the peak of a very high mountain one always sees the sun. Nirvana is not a paradise or some special place of happiness, but is in fact the condition beyond all dualistic concepts, including those of happiness and suffering.

When all our obstacles have been overcome, and we find ourselves in a state of total presence, the wisdom of enlightenment manifests spontaneously without limits, just like the infinite rays of the sun. The clouds have dissolved, and the sun is finally free to shine once again.

PART TWO

The Cuckoo of the
State of Presence

INTRODUCTION

The "Cuckoo of the State of Presence" (*Rig pa'i khu byug*) *is* one of the Dzogchen texts that was brought to Tibet in ancient times by Vairochana. The title of the text was invented by Vairochana as an epithet for the *Six Vajra Verses*, which belong to the category of Dzogchen writings known as "lung" (*lung*). Lung, which are part of the teachings originally transmitted by Garab Dorje, contain the essential points of one or more tantras.[1] The *Six Vajra Verses*, so called because they explain the primordial condition of the individual, sum up the essence of the *base, path,* and *fruit* of Dzogchen.

The story goes that Vairochana, who was also a great translator, was sent to Oddiyana by King Trisong Detsen to receive Dzogchen teachings, which up till then had not been introduced to Tibet. Padmasambhava had already transmitted Dzogchen teachings to his Tibetan disciples, but what he transmitted were mostly precepts linked to the methods of transformation of the Anuyoga.[2]

In Oddiyana Vairochana met the master Shri Singha, who taught him both sutras and esoteric teachings by day, and taught him Dzogchen by night, because of the ban on Dzogchen teachings imposed by the King of Oddiyana. Vairochana also translated a number of texts with the collaboration of Shri Singha, and it is said that he wrote them in goat's milk on white cotton in order to keep them secret. When he arrived back in his native country he began to transmit the Dzogchen teachings to the king and to a select few others. The text of the *Six Vajra Verses* was in fact the first text he introduced to Tibet, and so he gave it the name, *The Cuckoo of the State of Presence, a Sign of Good Fortune and Glory (bKra shis pa'i dpal rig pa'i khu byug).*[3]

In Tibet the cuckoo is considered to be a sign of good fortune and prosperity because it heralds the arrival of spring. When the Tibetan people heard the cuckoo's song they knew that the long cold winter was about to end, and that nature was about to awaken again. Thus the cuckoo's song is compared by Vairochana to the awakening of the presence of the primordial state (*rig pa*) that became possible with the introduction of the Dzogchen teachings to Tibet.

Over the course of the centuries the Dzogchen teachings have at times been the target of criticism and defamation aimed at them by some Tibetan scholars. One of the ways in which some of these people tried to prove that the Dzogchen texts were not authentic was by suggesting that there were errors of Sanskrit grammar in the titles of many Dzogchen tantras. What this in fact shows is that these denigrators of the Dzogchen teachings did not know of the existence of the language of Oddiyana, from which the tantras were translated into Tibetan by Vairochana and other masters. But the practitioners of Dzogchen have never had any interest in forming a sect, or in defending themselves and getting into arguments with others, because the principal thing in Dzogchen is the state of knowledge, which is not concerned with externals. Today, however, the historical authenticity of the Dzogchen texts can be proved, thanks to certain texts rediscovered among the Tun Huang manuscripts, which are considered original and authentic by all scholars.[4]

One of these rediscovered manuscripts in fact contains the *Cuckoo of the State of Presence*, which was found together with a commentary on it that was probably the work of Vairochana himself. These texts pass on to us some of the most ancient Dzogchen teachings, which reflect the original spirit of the oral tradition, in particular that of the Series of the Nature of the Mind.

The *Six Vajra Verses* are not just empty words. Through the understanding of their message, an uninterrupted line of masters, from the time of Garab Dorje on, has manifested knowledge of the primordial state. In the three parts of two lines each that make up the total of six lines, are to be found the principles of the base, the path, and the fruit, alongside a simultaneous explanation of the *way of seeing*, the *way of practicing*, and the *way of behaving* according to the Dzogchen teachings. The base is not something abstract. It is our own condition when we recognize our state. This is also true of the way of seeing of a Dzogchen practitioner, which is a point of view inseparable from real knowledge itself. The path is the means to develop this knowledge through the various methods of practice. And the fruit is the realization of uniting one's way of behaving with the state of presence, so that one's contemplation and one's daily activities are totally integrated. Through an understanding of the *Six Vajra Verses* we can gain direct access to the essence of Dzogchen.

Kuntuzangpo and Kuntuzangmo, Samantabhadra and Samantrabhadri,
representing the nondual state

Chapter Five
THE SIX VAJRA VERSES

sNa tshogs rang bzhin mi gnyis kyang
Cha shas nyid du spros dang bral
Ji bzhin ba zhes mi rtog kyang
rNam par snang mdzad kun tu bzang
Zin pas rtsol ba'i nad spangs te
lHun gyis gnas pas bzhag pa yin

The nature of phenomena is nondual,
but each one, in its own state, is beyond
the limits of the mind.
There is no concept that can define
the condition of "what is"
but vision nevertheless manifests:
all is good.
Everything has already been accomplished,
and so, having overcome the sickness of effort,
one finds oneself in the self-perfected state:
this is contemplation.

Chapter Six
THE BASE AND THE WAY OF SEEING

The nature of phenomena is nondual,
but each one, in its own state,
is beyond the limits of the mind.

The first two verses of the *Six Vajra Verses* explain the condition of the primordial *base*, and *way of seeing* in the Dzogchen teachings, pointing out that although there apparently exist an infinite number of things and phenomena, their real nature is one and the same. We can, for example, consider how many different types of people exist, and how many types of countries with all their different types of mountains, rivers, and vegetation. Then again, beyond our human dimension, we can imagine even more types of beings, whose worlds and what they contain are unknown to us.

All beings live within the various karmic visions that arise for them as a result of the passions they have accumulated. In the Sutras, 84,000 types of passion are described, which can cause the arising of an equal number of forms of existence. If we don't allow ourselves to get caught up in taking these numbers literally, we can nevertheless see that what is meant is that, just as there are infinite types of passions, so too there can be an equal number of karmic effects resulting from them.

The teachings explain that there exist three types of vision: the karmic or impure vision of ordinary beings; the vision of the "experiences" that arise to practitioners; and the pure vision of realized beings. Karmic vision is the illusory vision of beings in transmigration. It is called "illusory" because, depending on one's karma, it arises from a precise cause. The six principal passions are considered to be the fundamental causes of the six dimensions of existence. Attachment, jealousy, pride, mental obscuration, greed, and anger, give rise, respectively, to the karmic visions of the gods, the semi-gods, human beings, animals, hungry ghosts (*preta*), and hell beings. These dimensions are not worlds that can be found to be located in some area of the universe, but are karmic visions, which manifest according to the prevalence of one or other of the passions.

For we human beings, for example, the hell realm does not exist; but if we accumulate during this lifetime sufficient karma of the passion of anger, we can very easily be born in our next life in the karmic vision of hell. And the same is true if we accumulate the passions which cause births as other types of beings. Each one of them has a characteristic karmic vision, which lasts until the karma that produced it has been used up. A story used to give an example of this tells that there once came together, near a river, six different types of beings who each saw the river in a different way. The god among the six saw the river as nectar, the hungry ghost saw it as flaming lava, the human being as clear water, and so on. This example is used to make one understand that there does not exist one vision that is objectively real and concrete in the same way for all beings. If we were to offer a glass of water to drink to a hungry ghost, it would probably burn his throat.

By the term "vision of experience" what is meant is the manifestation of the results of practice. Through the practice of meditation, for example, there can arise the signs of the internal relaxation of the individual's five elements. Or, if one is practicing the methods of visualization found in tantrism, one can have experience of visions of such things as mandala or divinities. Since the individual has an infinite number of passions and functions of energy, these can, on the path, give rise to an infinite number of experiences.

When, on the other hand, the causes of karmic vision have been totally purified, one's vision does not disappear altogether, but rather manifests in its pure form, as the dimension of realized beings. In tantrism, for example, the final result of the practice is the transformation of the five passions into the five wisdoms. Thus the passions are not eliminated or annihilated, but are transformed in such a way that they can manifest in their purified, or essential, aspect. This pure vision of realized beings is not subject to the limits of space or time.

The three types of vision we have just discussed include all the infinite possibilities of forms of manifestation, but their inherent nature is not dual. This nature is the base, our fundamental condition, which is as clear, pure, and limpid as the capacity that enables a mirror to reflect. And just as different reflections appear in a mirror according to the secondary causes, so too the real condition of existence appears in different forms, either pure or impure, but its real nature does not change. That is why it is said that it is nondual.

"Nondual" is, in fact, a term that is used in Dzogchen a great deal, instead of the term "union." To understand why this is so, one needs to be aware that the word "union" implies that there exist two different things in the first place to be united, whereas "nondual" means that right from the beginning there is no concept of two separate things to be reunited. This is a way of explaining the base, but how can we enter into a real understanding of it? The fact is that the base cannot be understood through the intellect. Even if we think we have grasped the meaning of the word "nondual," we are really just fooling ourselves, because our mind is still caught up in the dualistic condition.

The mind is, by nature, limited. It does not have the capacity to think of two things at once, and exists at the relative level. When we think of everything as being nondual, our minds are in fact occupied in that moment with the concept. But that is not what is meant by "knowledge of the nondual state." Intellectual understanding and direct experiential knowledge are two very different things.

In Dzogchen the various methods of practice serve to favour the development of experiences, which are the principal means of developing one's state of knowledge, and of overcoming the obstacles which impede it. One can have an infinite variety of types of experiences linked to practice, but if they remain at the level of mental judgment they don't carry one towards true knowledge, but become obstacles in themselves. Only when one discovers that in all these different experiences there is the same state of presence, does one come to understand that which is beyond dualism.

When we practice contemplation, different experiences

can arise for us, but the presence of the state of contemplation never changes. That does not mean that one has to try in some way to cancel out or deny the experiences that may arise, but only that one should not mistake the experiences for the state of contemplation itself. Three fundamental types of experience are generally spoken of: the experiences of pleasure, of clarity, and of the absence of thoughts,[1] which correspond to the three aspects of the individual, body, voice and mind.

The experience of the absence of thoughts can imply both actual lack of thoughts, and a state in which thoughts, even if they arise, do not disturb one. This experience, which we can also define as a "void" state of mind, is a natural manifestation of the relaxation of the mind. The experience of clarity is linked to one's energy, to the aspect of the voice, and can manifest in various ways, through either sensations or visions. An example would be the pure apparition of the mandala of a divinity. The experience of pleasure is linked to the physical level of the individual, to the body. When one practises meditation on the calm state for a long time, for example, one can experience a sensation that one's body is no longer there, or else a sensation of great pleasure such as that of finding oneself in the middle of a cloud up in empty space.

These are examples of the infinite types of experience that can manifest through the practice. Finding oneself in the state of contemplation means relaxing completely, so if one becomes attached to pleasurable experiences, or conditioned by a vision or a state without thoughts, this will have the opposite effect to that desired. In order to relax, one should not get "blocked" by an experience, mistaking it for the state of contemplation. This can be a great obstacle to realization. If a practitioner remains absorbed for days and days in a state of pleasure, or of voidness, without maintaining the presence of contemplation, this is like falling asleep in an experience. This happens when the experiences are mistaken for one's true destination.

There is a great deal of difference between a sensation of pleasure and one of voidness, but the inherent nature of both the two experiences is one and the same. When we are in a state of voidness and have not lost consciousness, there is a presence that continues all the time, a presence which is just the same in an experience of pleasurable sensation. This presence is unique and beyond the mind. It is a nondual state which is the basis of all the infinite forms of manifestation, and in order to re-acquire it, direct transmission from the master is indispensable.

The second verse of the Six Vajra Verses which reads: "but each one, in its own state, is beyond the limits of the mind," means that, even if the nature of existence is nondual, everything manifests distinctly as the energy of the primordial state. The true state of every single thing that manifests as an object is actually beyond all definitions and beyond all concepts. We have, earlier in this book, compared the "tsel" aspect of the manifestation of our energy to a crystal ball, because crystal is transparent, and its nature is clear, pure, and limpid. And we have already noted how, when the secondary cause of the sun's rays is present, infinite rays of rainbow light spread out from the crystal. This example is given to show how both the pure vision of a realized being which manifests in the form of mandala and divinities, and the impure vision of ordinary beings who are limited by dualism and by karma, manifest from the individual's own state in just the same way that the rays manifest from a crystal when the sun strikes it. Thus, in the same way that the thousands of forms and colors manifest from the crystal, infinite varieties of phenomena can arise in relation to our own primordial state.

There is a saying in Dzogchen which goes, "Solid objects are pure right from the beginning," which means that the inherent nature of any kind of apparently manifest object is void and fundamentally pure. For example, even if we, looking with our "common karmic vision," would see a yellow tent, an animal or another type of being would not see the same object in the same way, because such a being lacks the causes of human karmic vision. Thus there does not exist one solid, unchangeable, universal vision of things. All that appears to us as a dimension of objects is not, in fact, really something concrete at all, but is an aspect of our own primordial state appearing to us. So the real nature of objects cannot be defined, which is why the *Six Vajra Verses* say that their nature is "beyond the limits of the mind."

When we really find ourselves in this nondual state, at the center of the manifestation of all the infinite number of possible phenomena, then we can be said to be really beginning to relax. Until one does truly discover this state, whatever relaxation of body, voice, or mind one does succeed in finding remains only provisional. One might manage to relax one's body by lying down, or relax one's energy by doing breathing practices, but these are only partial relaxations, because to have their effect, such exercises must be repeated every day. And then again, sometimes, when we are very agitated, even if we try to relax, we will not succeed in doing so, because we remain completely dependent on all the various circumstances related to our situation.

Everybody would ideally like to live a peaceful and relaxed life. Even people who don't follow any particular religious system, and who perhaps would say they don't believe in anything at all, would like to live a peaceful life. So the teachings are not something of interest only to those who feel themselves to be "spiritual," but are really something useful to anyone at all who would like to live in a more relaxed way, and thus be able to resolve their everyday problems more easily.

We generally have very many kinds of problems and conflicts, and in fact the Buddha himself pointed out that the very nature of samsara is suffering. If we observe our own condition for a day, a week, or a month, we will surely notice that we are never completely free of suffering. And if we don't know how to relax, the situation is clearly worse, because we aggravate it even more with our agitation. When we are agitated even the simplest things become difficult, so it is very important to learn to relax, but without there being any intention to relax. When we find a state beyond all our usual tensions, everything relaxes automatically. In fact, in the true state of contemplation, there is nothing to relax, because the nature of that state is in itself relaxed.

Dzogchen could be defined as a way to relax completely. This can be clearly understood from the terms used to denote the state of contemplation, such as, "leave it just as it is" *(cog bzhag)*, "cutting loose one's tension" *(khregs chod)*, "beyond effort" *(rtsol bral)*, and so on. Some scholars have classified Dzogchen as a "direct path," comparing it to teachings such as Zen, where this expression is often used. In Dzogchen texts, however, the phrases "direct path" and "nongradual path" *(cig car)* are never used, because the concept of a "direct path" implies necessarily that there must be, on the one hand, a place from which one departs, and on the other, a place where one arrives. But in Dzogchen there is the single principle of the state of knowledge, and if one possesses this state one discovers that right from the beginning one is already there where one wants to arrive. For this reason the state is said to be "self-perfected" *(lhun grub)*.

In the Mahayana Sutras, ten *bhumi*, or levels of Bodhisattva's spiritual realization, are spoken of as leading gradually to total enlightenment. These grades of realization are based on the level of the purification of subtle obstacles to knowledge achieved by the practitioner. But in the nondual condition there do not really exist levels or stages of realization; from this point of view there is only *bhumi*, which is the state of knowledge itself.

The state of knowledge arises and matures through relaxation, but by "relaxing" we don't mean just doing nothing at all. Sometimes people misunderstand the principle of "not-correcting" anything in Dzogchen and they allow themselves to become distracted. But the practice of Dzogchen means that one learns to relax whilst all the time maintaining one's presence in whatever circumstances one finds oneself in. Thus, in a state of total completeness, one remains relaxed and present in relation to all the infinite manifestations of energy that may arise. To practice Dzogchen it is not necessary to study the ideas of a religious or philosophical tradition. Dzogchen can perfectly well be understood without the use of a lot of complicated terms and expressions. For example, we use the name "Dzogchen" because it points to the total (*chen*) completeness (*dzog*) of the state of the individual, but it would make no difference if we were to use some other term. The real principle is, after all, transmission of a state of knowledge that can open and awaken the individual, and not how one defines the spiritual tradition involved.

Some people think that it is not indispensable that one has a master, and feel that, in order to be able to practice, the instructions they might find in a book are enough. But a book, as well as not being able to contain the living transmission of a teaching, also cannot contain examples and explanations suitable for every type of person. A master, collaborating with the disciples, helps them to find the state of contemplation through experience of body, voice, and mind, and teaches many methods for developing the state of knowledge. Knowing the particular character of each disciple, the master can advise him or her which methods will be most suitable for them.

These first two verses also explain the way of seeing in Dzogchen, because the nondual nature of all phenomena they refer to is not something external to the individual, but is really the true condition of every individual him or herself. Thus, if we keep on looking for it outside ourselves, how will we ever be able to understand the primordial state? All that we perceive as external through the net of dualism is in fact just the result of the separation between subject and object that we ourselves, with our minds, have created. It is our own minds that give rise to all our judgments, attachments, and karma, and to understand the nonduality spoken of in the *Six Vajra Verses* we simply need to be aware of the principle that what we perceive as our vision is in fact the manifest potentiality of our own primordial state.

In the various traditions of Tibetan Buddhism, what is generally meant by the *way of seeing* is the particular philosophical theory on which that particular school is based. All the schools of Tibetan Buddhism accept the works of Nagarjuna, the culmination of Mahayana Buddhist philosophy, as containing the supreme way of seeing, which is known as the Middle Way. According to this philosophical system it is impossible, from the point of view of the ultimate reality whose nature is indescribable voidness, to affirm anything at all as being absolutely true. By means of this kind of reasoning, with ruthless logic, Nagarjuna overturned all the extremist views of all the other philosophical schools of his day.

Over the course of the following centuries, however, there arose among the Tibetan schools variations in the interpretation of Nagarjuna's philosophy which gave rise to endless doctrinal controversies and disputes. Every school tried to defend and sustain its own characteristic way of seeing on the basis of logic and speculation. But this attitude has nothing at all in common with the nondual way of seeing, which is beyond reasoning and discussion.

Buddhist philosophy in general is based on the concept of the *two truths*, relative and absolute. The latter corresponds to the absolute condition, which is void and nondual, while the former corresponds to everything which arises in the relative condition of existence. In actual practice, it is considered that when one is in a state of meditation, sitting with one's back straight, then one is in the absolute condition. But when one's session of meditation is finished and one re-enters the activities of daily life, then one is in the relative condition. It is as if one were to have two legs, one of the absolute truth, and the other of the relative truth, to proceed along the path to realization, which is defined as the union of the two truths. But in Dzogchen, right from the beginning this concept of two truths does not exist, and the nondual state is introduced as the foundation of both the way of seeing and of the way of practicing.

In Dzogchen one's way of seeing must not be that of one who looks outwards through a pair of spectacles. Even if through their lenses one might be able to see clearly thousands of shapes and colors, the direction one is looking in is still mistaken. For this reason the mirror is used as an example, because if we look in a mirror we see our own face, and even if we don't like the way it looks, we have to accept it. This is the only way we can discover something deeper, and to begin to really understand it.

The way of seeing can help us a great deal in developing a correct understanding of the base, but it is nevertheless still easy for our knowledge to remain merely intellectual. This is an obstacle that is very subtle and difficult to remove, because often we do not even notice it. There are, in general, two kinds of obstacles a practitioner can encounter, obstacles of the passions, and obstacles of knowledge. Obstacles of the passions, of negative karma, and so on, are relatively easy to discover. But obstacles of knowledge are subtle and can even seriously hinder very advanced practitioners. Even if one has, for example, overcome one's attachment and one's passions and has gained a certain level of stability in one's meditation, as long as one can still be caught up in any idea or concept about knowledge itself, one is still automatically shut out of the path to realization. Thus, the way one understands the base is extremely important in Dzogchen.

Some people, when they follow a master, blindly believe everything he or she says, without verifying it through the methods of practice. But then there are others who think it is always necessary to debate and discuss everything. But the truth is that one will never actually resolve anything through either reasoning about everything or through accepting passively everything the master says as if he or she was a general. All we need to do is to try to "taste" that which the master is communicating, so that we can truly discover the state of knowledge in ourselves. When the master explains something, he is not doing so just to put forward an idea of his own, but to provide the disciples with the means to understand their own nature.

The master explains, teaches, helps, and so on, but cannot accomplish the miracle of illuminating, or transforming someone else's condition. Some people are convinced that extraordinary masters exist who are capable of making a gift of enlightenment to others, but no one can do that. The power of the master is to explain and make something understood, transmitting the state of knowledge in different ways. When the student, applying the practices, enters into

*Vairochana, translator of the Six Vajra Verses
from the language of Oddiyana into Tibetan*

the state of knowledge, then one can indeed say that the master has accomplished a miracle. In fact the Buddha himself said, "I can show you the path, but realization depends on you yourself."

Sometimes, however, it is not possible to transmit the teachings because there is not sufficient capacity or participation on the part of those who want to receive them. A few years ago, for example, I went to the region of Nepal where the Sherpa people live. Many Sherpas came to see me, since they had heard me spoken of as the reincarnation of another master.[2] When they came into the room where I was, they offered me rice, money, and the traditional white scarf used for greeting people. Then they asked me for a blessing and went away. Not one of them asked me for any teaching, and this is typical of what we mean when we say someone has a passive attitude towards the teachings.

The Buddha said that realization depends on us, ourselves. He was totally enlightened, omniscient, and full of compassion. He was not indifferent to the suffering of other beings. So why wouldn't he have performed the miracle of enlightening all the beings in transmigration, if such a thing were possible? But the fact is that if it was not possible even for the Buddha to do such a thing, then it is not possible for anyone to do it. Thus we need to be active towards the teachings ourselves, really applying them in our lives.

To enter and remain stable in the state of contemplation, so as to be able to integrate that state with all our daily activities, a great deal of experience of practice may be necessary, but we should not allow ourselves to become worried about all the different methods, or let them condition us. It can happen that, after one has received an initiation, for example, one makes a commitment to do that practice every day. Maybe for the first few days one has no difficulty in fulfilling this promise, but after a little while conflicts may begin to arise, because one has forced oneself, as a result of one's limited idea of being obliged to sit down to practice, to do this every day whether the circumstances are suitable or not. In Dzogchen this attitude is considered unfavorable to one's progress in the practice, because if one becomes over-dependent on the methods of the teaching, one does not reap the benefit of the essence of the state of relaxation.

I have in my wardrobe, for example, many types of clothes, but that doesn't mean that I have of necessity to put them all on every day. Rather it's a matter of my choosing the clothes each time that are most suited to the circumstances I find myself in. In the same way, there exist in the teachings thousands of methods, but if one understands the principle of contemplation, it's not important which of these methods one uses.

The Dzogchen teachings are based on four points, the first of which is that, "It is based on the real, and not on the conventional, meaning." The "conventional meaning" is the way knowledge is communicated by entering into the mentality or the customs of those who are to receive it, which is the way the Buddha taught when he used notions and concepts belonging to the Indian culture of his time, even though he was perfectly aware of the illusory nature of all concepts. His discourses had as their only goal the aim of transmitting the state which is beyond concepts, which is the "real meaning" referred to in this first point. Dzogchen is said to be based on the real meaning, because right from the beginning it teaches one to find oneself in one's natural condition, without changing or altering it.

The second point is that, "It is based on the individual, and not on the teachings." In the path of renunciation, the person on the path makes themselves subordinate to the teaching. Not having the capacity to assume responsibility for oneself, one makes the decision to observe certain rules, accepting that one will not commit those actions that are prohibited by the monastic code. But Dzogchen is based on the individual, because in Dzogchen the fundamental thing is to understand one's own capacity and to know how to use those methods that are most suited to it.

The third point says: "It is based on primordial wisdom and not on the mind." The mind is the basis of dualism and of all our conflicts, whereas primordial wisdom is the nature of the state of presence, the knowledge that arises as a result of the transmission from the master, and is developed through the practice of contemplation.

The last point is that, "It is based on the meaning and not on the words," which means that one should try to enter into the real sense of what the master communicates, and not remain caught up in just the literal meaning of the words. A term such as *bodhichitta*, for example, has different meanings depending on whether it is found in the context of the Sutras, the Tantras, or Dzogchen.

The principle of the base is not peculiar to the Dzogchen teachings, but is found in all the Buddhist traditions. At the sutra level the base means the knowledge of the two truths, relative and absolute, which correspond to the concepts of the "mind" and "the nature of the mind." The path in the Sutras is the two accumulations, of merit and of wisdom, the first of which is linked to the relative condition through working with the three aspects of the individual in the following way: with the body one carries out virtuous actions, with the voice one recites mantras of purification, and with the mind one cultivates thoughts of compassion for others. Virtuous actions have the power to diminish the individual's obstacles, creating the conditions necessary for the path of the accumulation of wisdom.

The accumulation of wisdom involves knowledge of the absolute condition, through knowledge of the state of contemplation. This is considered the fundamental path even in the Sutras, and the Buddha himself pointed out that "A person who remains in contemplation for the amount of time it takes an ant to travel from the tip of his nose to his forehead will accumulate much more wisdom than another person who, even at the cost of great self-sacrifice, makes offerings to the Buddha and the divinities for a whole lifetime." Nevertheless, in the Sutras it is generally considered that, since it is not easy to understand and apply the path of wisdom directly, one should in fact practice purification and the accumulation merit.

It is said that when the Buddha tried for the first time to communicate the state of knowledge to his disciples, since none of them understood him, he told them, "I have found a path to the state of knowledge that is profound and clear, beyond concepts and beyond all explanations. But when I have tried to communicate it, no one understands it. So I will therefore go to live alone in the forest, where I shall meditate in solitude." This shows how difficult it is to communicate the path of wisdom, and a Dzogchen text written in verse[3] actually says, "To explain this state, even the Buddha's tongue is weak."

Chapter Seven
THE PATH AND THE WAY OF PRACTICING

There is no concept that can define the condition of
    "what is"
but vision nevertheless manifests: all is good.

The practice of Dzogchen is said to be "beyond effort," and indeed one does not need to create, modify, or change anything, but only to find oneself in the true condition of "what is." But it can happen that a phrase intended to indicate a state beyond concepts just becomes another concept in itself, in the same way that if you ask a person their name and they reply that they have no name, you will then perhaps mistakenly call them "No name."

    The next two verses of the *Six Vajra Verses* explain the meaning of the path and the practice of Dzogchen. The expression "what is" *(ji bzhin ba)* is used a great deal in ancient Dzogchen texts, and it is synonymous with "uncorrected" *(ma bcos pa)* and other terms that denote the true and unaltered, unmodified and uncorrected state. Correcting, modifying and so on are all characteristic functions of our dualistic minds, and so finding oneself in an uncorrected state means going beyond the mind. In Dzogchen this is true not only at the final stage of the practice, as in other traditions, but rather, right from the very beginning one has to try to enter into knowledge of the state of "what is."

In tantrism, the introduction to the original nature of the mind is the last stage of the practice, after the developing and completion stages. But in Dzogchen this condition is introduced directly, not only at the level of mind, but also at the levels of voice and body, because, to be integrated with contemplation, all the aspects of our existence must be in this uncorrected state.

In *The Great Space of Vajrasattva (rDo rje sems dpa' nam mkha' che)*,[1] one of the principal texts of the Series of the Nature of the Mind, it is written that, "To correct the condition of the body in order to find a state of contemplation does not apply in Dzogchen. Controlling the position of one's body and keeping a straight back are not contemplation, but can in fact become an obstacle to contemplation." As a result of such statements some people have accused Dzogchen of denying the value of sitting meditation, or of controlling one's breathing or body position, and so on. But Dzogchen does not deny anything at all, and when leaving the body "uncontrolled" is spoken of, what is meant is simply allowing the body to remain in an authentic, uncorrected condition, in which it is not necessary to modify or improve anything. This is because, since all our attempts at correcting the body come from the reasoning mind, they are all false and artificial.

In the Series of Secret Instructions, four ways of continuing in contemplation, known as the four ways of "leaving it just as it is,"[2] are explained. The first, which refers to the body, is said to be "like a mountain." What this refers to is that, even though a mountain can be higher or lower, or of different shape, it is something that nevertheless always remains stable, and never changes its position. In the same way, in the course of even a single day we assume different positions according to the varying circumstances we find ourselves in, and all these positions are equally suitable for contemplation, without the need to alter them. If the position I find myself in happens to be that of lying down, at the moment in which I find myself in the state of "what is," then that itself is my natural position, just like the settled position of a mountain. It is not necessary that I immediately get up, straighten my back, and cross my legs. The same is also true if I find myself in contemplation at the moment of drinking a cup of coffee. It's not necessary for me to rush off to my room, close the door, and sit down in meditation. All the above points are useful in learning how to integrate contemplation with daily life.

In order to be able to truly integrate one's practice with one's life, a few sessions of sitting meditation a day are simply not enough, because we live a twenty-four hour day, and an hour or two of practice just won't give the right results. "Integrating," on the other hand, means understanding the condition of "what is" in relation to life itself, without correcting it, so that every circumstance of one's life becomes an occasion for practice.

One might then very well ask, "Since in Dzogchen it is taught that one should not correct anything, does this mean that it is useless to carry out practices of breathing, visualization, and so on, which are actually based on correcting something or other?" But in Dzogchen "not correcting" does not mean either negating or undertaking any method of practice. Rather the practitioner must be open and relaxed in relation to the various methods, and know how to use them, without being conditioned by them.

Sometimes it may be that such great importance will be given to the details of the position of one's body, of one's hands, and so on, and to the color and form of the divinity to be visualized, that the real meaning of what one is actually doing is overlooked. Position, breathing, and visualization, working with the three aspects of body, voice, and mind, are just the means to enable us to enter the relaxed state of contemplation. There exist thousands of methods of practice, many of which may seem much like one another, so if one only looks at the externals, rather than the essential meaning, one may very well be troubled by doubts and contradictions. But all such problems and conflicts arise from the mind, which is like a limited person who is aided and abetted by five even more limited persons—the five senses. When one truly knows the state of contemplation, however, beyond effort, and beyond judgment, one will also be able to overcome these problems in relation to the methods of practice.

In the Tantras, the method for arriving at the uncorrected state is that of transformation, through visualization of the pure dimension. Lets's take the example of the *Hevajra Tantra*. Hevajra is the name given to the pure manifestation of a particular realized being, as it was received by a certain master. When one receives transmission of *Hevajra Tantra*, one applies the vision of the transformation every day, using the Hevajra mantra, to integrate the visualization with one's own energy. Then, at a certain moment, the vision of the transformation ceases to depend on one's visualization and becomes a manifestation of one's innate clarity. Everything becomes reintegrated with that clarity, in the contemplation of the Mahamudra. When one reaches this state, the transformation is no longer the fundamental thing. One can understand this very well if one reads some of the poetry of the mahasiddhas, or their biographies.

One of the most famous practitioners of the *Hevajra Tantra* was the mahasiddha Virupa. He was originally a great scholar, a pandit, but he later became a tantric practitioner. For years and years he applied himself to the method of transformation of Hevajra, in particular reciting the mantra of Damema (bDag med ma), the consort of Hevajra. The story goes that one day, while he was in a state of contemplation of total clarity, he suddenly got up and threw his *mala*,[3] which he usually held in his hands while reciting the mantra, into the toilet. Then when he got back to his room, he threw the mandala offering he had prepared for the practice onto the ground and went away, never to return. Virupa had awakened, but everyone thought he had gone crazy.

Sometimes realized beings, like crazy people, act in a way that is beyond the "normal" limits of conventional behavior; but the fact is, we are the crazy ones, "maddened" by the five passions and all our attachments. Not noticing this, we call those who don't behave in a way we consider normal, "crazy." For this reason many masters, such as Drukpa Kunlay ('Brug pa kun legs), who had a life-style that was beyond limits, have been called "crazy yogis."

So we have seen that in tantrism, too, at the end of the practice, one breaks the imaginary construction of the transformation process, and reaches a state of integration with pure manifestation, beyond concepts. To reach this level, however, many years of practice are necessary in retreat. But Dzogchen, the "path of self-liberation," is based on the principle of knowledge, not in the sense of making a mental decision once and for all to know something and then never to modify it, but in the sense of really and truly discovering the presence of the primordial state.

The practice of Dzogchen may begin with doing fixation on an object, in order to calm one's thoughts. Then one relaxes the fixation, dissolving the dependence on the object, and one fixes one's gaze in open space. Then, when one succeeds in making the calm state stable, it is important to work with the movement of one's thoughts and one's energy, integrating this movement with the presence of contemplation. At this point one is ready to apply contemplation in one's daily life. The system of practice just described is characteristic of the Series of the Nature of the Mind, but that is not to say that in Dzogchen one must necessarily begin with fixation and meditation on a calm state. In the Series of Primordial Space, and the Series of Secret Instructions, for example, one enters directly into the practice of contemplation. Particularly in the former, there are very precise instructions on how to find the pure state of contemplation. In the latter, on the other hand, the explanations are mainly concerned with how one continues in contemplation in all circumstances.

The practice of contemplation is concisely explained in the line that reads, "but vision nevertheless manifests: all is good."[4] Even if the condition of "what is" cannot be grasped with the mind, the whole manifestation of the primordial state, including our karmic vision, does nevertheless exist. All the various aspects of forms, colours, and so on, continue to arise without interruption. When we find ourselves in contemplation, this doesn't mean that our impure vision just disappears and pure vision manifests instead. If we have a physical body, there is a karmic cause for that, so there would be no sense in trying to abandon or deny the situation we find ourselves in. We just need to be aware of it. If we have a vision of the material, physical level of existence, which is the cause of so very many problems, we need to understand that this vision is only the gross aspect of the colours, which are the essence of the elements. Water, for example, is the material manifestation of the colour white, the essence of the element water, which has become what it is for us in its substantial, material form through our karma and our ignorance. When we finally discover the principle of this manifestation into material forms, however, we can reverse the process, so as to cause water to return to its subtle state as luminous essence. The principal means to accomplish this reversal is through contemplation, bringing about the reintegration of one's own energy with that of the material dimension.

"All is good," which is the translation into Tibetan of the name Samantabhadra, the primordial Dharmakaya Buddha, means that there is nothing to modify or eliminate in one's vision, which is perfect just as it is. When one is in the nondual state, even thousands of apparitions cannot disturb one's contemplation. But "good" is not here being regarded as something "positive," which is then being set in opposition to something considered "negative." What is being referred to is a state in which there is nothing negative to reject and nothing positive to accept. All that manifests is beyond both good and bad, and is like an ornament to one's own primordial state.

In Dzogchen it is not necessary to transform impure vision into pure vision, working with one's imagination. All one's vision is an inherent quality of one's own natural clarity. If we see a house made of stone, and we try to imagine it transformed into a dimension of light, we are just playing with our minds, because the house as it is, even if it is a part of our karmic vision, is really a manifestation of our own clarity. So why should we block it, or transform it? Problems only arise when we enter into judging whether the house is beautiful or ugly, big or small, and so on. Then, with our reasoning minds, it is very easy to enter into action and produce karma.

Machig Labdron (Ma gcig lab sgron), in her teachings on the practice of the Chod *(gcod)*, explained that there are four "devils," or obstacles, that impede one's path to realization. The first is called "the devil which blocks (the senses)."[5] When we see a beautiful object, if the mind enters into judgment in relation to it, desire arises and one falls prey to one's passions. What's at the bottom of this? First our eyes perceive the object, without there being any concept of beautiful or ugly. Then the mind begins to function and the direct perception of the senses becomes blocked. Thus, the perceived object becomes a hindrance, or "devil." When perception is not blocked by mental judgment, however, the vision self-liberates, like a knot in the body of a snake untying itself of itself.

If something wonderful appears before us, but we don't enter into judgment of it, it remains part of our clarity. The same is true if something horrible appears to us. So why do we develop desire for the one and aversion for the other? Clarity does not belong to our reasoning mind but to the pure presence of the primordial state, which is beyond both good and evil, and, in Tibet, developed practitioners of the Chod were called in to help when there was an epidemic or an outbreak of a contagious disease, because, having gone completely beyond any concept of "good" and "evil" or "pure" and "impure," they were immune to all kinds of contagion.

It is important to maintain one's presence in contemplation, without correcting the body, the voice, or the mind. One needs to find oneself in a relaxed condition, but the senses must be present and alert, because they are the gates to clarity. Letting go of all tension with regard to bodily position, breathing, and thoughts, just maintaining a vivid presence, one relaxes without any effort at all.

When one begins to practice, it may seem that the confusion of one's thoughts is increasing, but this is really due to the relaxation of the mind. In fact, this movement of thoughts has always existed; it's just that now one has become aware of it, because the mind has become more clear, in the same way that, as long as the sea is agitated, one cannot see what is on the seabed, but when it becomes calm one can see what was down there all along.

When we become conscious of the movement of our thoughts, we must learn to integrate them with presence, without following them or allowing ourselves to become distracted by them. What do we mean by "becoming distracted"? If I see a person and take an immediate dislike to them, this means I have allowed myself to get caught up in mental judgment; that is to say, I have become distracted. If I maintain presence, on the other hand, why on earth should I take a dislike to someone I see? That person is also actually a part of my own clarity. If I really understand this, all my tensions and conflicts will dissolve, and everything will settle into a state of complete relaxation.

There are two principal defects often encountered in practice, and they are sleepiness and agitation. Sometimes, for example, when we are engaged in practice we either get drowsy, or else we find that we are so agitated that our thoughts never give us any peace for a moment, and it seems impossible to find a calm state. There are practices that one can apply as an antidote to these problems, but if we know how to relax in ourselves we can overcome these difficulties naturally without such effort.

A person who is beginning to practice usually prefers to withdraw to a secluded place, because they need to find a state of calm and mental balance. But when one begins to have real experience of the state of contemplation one needs to integrate it with all one's daily activities, of walking, talking, eating, and so on. A Dzogchen practitioner never needs to give up on society and retire to meditate on a mountain top. This is especially inappropriate in our modern society, in which we all have to work to eat and live normally. If we know how to integrate our contemplation into our daily lives, however, we will manifest progress in our practice just the same.

Practicing means integrating oneself with vision. The term "vision" here includes all our sense perceptions. Whether I am in a room listening to pleasant music, or somewhere where there is a lot of deafening noise, such as in a factory, should make no difference, because it is all part of vision. Whether I smell the delicate scent of a rose, or the stink of a toilet, these too are part of vision, and in contemplation this vision is perceived as the manifestation of the energy of the primordial state, with nothing to be rejected or accepted. Thus, the essence of the practice is to find oneself in a state of relaxed presence, integrated with whatever perception may arise.

The knowledge of contemplation is transmitted directly from the master to the disciple, and in Dzogchen, explaining and making the real meaning understood are part of the transmission. For this, it is not necessary to prepare a mandala or touch the disciple's head with a vase.[6] These are elements of ritual which belong to the tantric tradition. Nor is it even necessary to receive the vow of refuge, which is one of the fundamental pillars of Buddhism. Because of this, some people who have received transmission of the Dzogchen teachings feel uneasy because they haven't taken this refuge vow.[7] But what such an attitude shows is that they are ignorant of the real meaning of refuge, because even in the Buddhist Sutras it is stated that the ultimate refuge is the essence of the *tathagatas*, which is the state of primordial enlightenment.

Nowadays, however, the vow of refuge has become common place even in the West. After the ritual ceremony of refuge, during which a lock of one's hair is cut and one is given a Tibetan name, a person will probably think to themselves, "I have received refuge; now I am a Buddhist." But there is, in fact, no need to feel oneself to be a "Buddhist." Our condition of "what is" is sufficient just as it is, so why must one become something other than what one already is?

If we take a vow this means that we do not have the capacity to govern ourselves. But our capacity is relative to the circumstances we find ourselves in, and can be improved. So the first thing one needs to do is to discover what one's own capacity is, and then, according to one's needs, try to increase one's capacity by means of the various methods of practice. There are, for example, very many purification practices whose purpose is to remove the obstacles to clarity, and the disciple will work with one or other of these methods of purification selected to suit his or her own particular condition. The master cannot decide for the disciple which practice will be most suitable, but can only give some advice and suggestions on this, to help the disciple to see more clearly into him or herself, and thus to become more aware and self-reliant.

The situation in the path of renunciation is very different from that which we have just described, because the fundamental aspect of that path is that one follows rules of behaviour that limit one's actions of body, voice, and mind. The rules of any religious tradition, however, can never be universal, and are dependent on circumstances and on time.

A rule that today seems valid, may tomorrow, with the passing of time and the changing of people's habits, become no longer relevant. The rules of the Vinaya, for example, undoubtedly arose to govern aspects of the behaviour of the disciples of the Buddha that were considered incorrect in relation to the environment in which they lived. Suppose, for example, that some of the Buddha's disciples went around naked, and were thus thought of badly by the inhabitants of a nearby village. Then the Buddha would pronounce a rule declaring that, "The disciples of the Buddha must not go around naked." The 252 principal rules of the Vinaya were all made in this way. So it is obvious that some of these rules, which arose in relation to the climatic conditions of India, would be impossible to apply in a country such as Tibet if they were not adapted to suit the different climate and diet to be found there.

In Dzogchen one learns to become responsible for oneself without following rules. A person who follows rules is like a blind person who needs someone to guide them in order to be able to walk. For this reason it is said that a Dzogchen practitioner must open his or her eyes to discover their condition, so that they will no longer be dependent on anyone or anything.

Some people, because they are not satisfied by their ordinary relationship with the master, think to themselves, "The master is just an ordinary person who eats spaghetti and drinks wine just like me. But I want to enter into direct contact with the Buddha or with Padmasambhava." We all have this attitude a little deep down in ourselves, because the principal cause of birth in the human realm is pride. But it is, in reality, very difficult to enter into contact with the Buddha if we do not recognize the Buddha in our master; in fact, the true Buddha, for the disciple, is the master.

In the *Abhisamayalankara,* a commentary on the *Prajña-paramita-sutra,* it is written, "Even if the rays of the sun are strong, they will not produce a fire if there is no lens [to focus them]. Even if the thousand Buddhas are full of wisdom, one cannot receive it except through a master."

In the *"Cuckoo" Tantra* it is written that, "Knowledge of the condition of 'what is' is introduced by the master through the transmission, and developed through contemplation. The value of the master is like that of the mineral used to clean gold." In Tibet a mineral was used to clean off, from the surface of gold, the substances covering it. When this mineral comes into contact with the gold its real colour reappears. The gold is a symbol, in this example, of that which is called Dzogchen, the primordial state which is our own inherent condition, self-perfected right from the very beginning. The substances covering the gold represent the obstacles and the confusion of the relative condition which prevent the knowledge of the primordial state from manifesting itself. And the mineral which cleans the gold, making its true color reappear, is the power of the transmission from the master which enables us to rediscover our own condition. Even if the gold, when covered with grime, appears to be only a rock or a lump of earth, its real quality is nevertheless always the same and only needs to be rediscovered.

The master is inseparable from the state of knowledge, and in Dzogchen one of the fundamental practices for developing contemplation is, in fact, the Guru Yoga, or the "Union with the Master." The real purpose of this practice is to keep the transmission from the master alive and ever-present in the disciple's life. Another fundamental aspect of the teachings, which derives from the Tantras, is the *samaya,* or "promise," which is the equivalent in tantrism of the vows in the sutra teachings. When one receives an initiation, for example, one promises to carry out the transformation practice daily, reciting the corresponding mantra at least three or seven times. On top of this commitment, there are also many other related samaya which must be observed. But in Dzogchen the only samaya involved is to find oneself in the condition of "what is," as it is. All the rest, that is to say all the judgments and creations of the mind, all our limits, and so on, all these are false and superfluous. Without becoming distracted, one tries to find oneself at all times in a relaxed state.

When we are in the state of contemplation, even if a thousand thoughts arise, we don't follow them, but just remain observing everything that happens. This is what is meant by presence. Finding oneself in the state of "what is" means maintaining continuous presence. So the samaya of Dzogchen means not becoming distracted, and just that. But that doesn't mean that if one does become distracted one has broken one's samaya. What one has to do is notice what has happened, and try once again not to become distracted.

There are two ways of not becoming distracted. The highest of these is when one's capacity of contemplation is sufficiently developed for one to succeed in integrating all one's actions with the state of presence. This is the final arrival point of the practice, and is known as Great Contemplation. But as long as one is not able to reach this level, there is a way of not becoming distracted that is more linked to the mind, in which one has to maintain a minimum of attention. This is not true contemplation, because there is still a certain amount of intentionality, of working actively with the reasoning mind, involved. But this stage is nevertheless very useful to help us to develop the state of presence.

If we notice any tension arising, it is important to relax it, but without entering into an attitude of struggling with our distraction, which would bring the opposite effect to that desired. In our daily lives we need to remember to always relax, because that is the key to everything for us. Let's take a concrete example: Suppose that while we are sitting in one room, the idea comes into our heads to go and get an object that is in another room. As soon as this thought arises, we recognize it, and are aware of it, but we don't try to block it, or to make it dissolve. Without becoming distracted, maintaining a relaxed presence, we get up and go into the other room, trying to remain present in everything that we do. This is an extremely important practice, which requires neither a particular position and control of the breathing, nor any visualization. All one has to do is to remain present and relaxed.

At the beginning it may not be easy to maintain one's presence, but little by little one can succeed in integrating it with the movements of one's body. It's the same with the voice: while talking, discussing something, or singing, one should try to maintain one's presence for as long as possible. And then, as far as the mind is concerned, it's the same with that: one should try to remain present while the processes of reasoning, or imagining, and so on, are going on. One might think, "How on earth can I integrate the process of reasoning with presence if it's the mind that's the cause of distraction?" But the mind is really just like a reflection that arises in a mirror. If one re-enters the mirror's inherent capacity to reflect, the reflection will no longer remain something external to oneself, perceived dualistically. When one finds oneself in the condition of the nature of the mirror, every aspect of one's body, voice, and mind is a manifestation of the wisdom of the state of presence. Wisdom is beyond the mind, but when we say it is "beyond" it, this does not mean that it has no relationship at all with it. In fact the relationship between one's inherent wisdom and the reasoning mind is the same as that between a mirror and the reflections that arise in it.

When one speaks of the way one continues in contemplation, explanations are given of the various experiences with which contemplation is linked. All the various experiences that arise in practice are related to the condition of our actual existence, which can be said, in general, to have two aspects or characteristics, the "calm state" and the "movement." When a thought arises and we observe it to discover where it arose from, where it stays, and where it goes to, we don't find anything concrete at all. Even if our thoughts apparently do seem to exist, when we observe them, they just disappear without leaving a trace. This situation is the same, too, in relation to the voice and the body. If one has a headache, for example, and observes where the pain arises from and where it goes when it disappears, one can't come to any real conclusion. This condition of voidness in relation to the body corresponds to the calm state in relation to the mind.

But even if our thoughts disappear in this way, they nevertheless then arise again without interruption. This is what is called the "movement," which is the functioning of clarity. In Dzogchen it is necessary to learn to work with this "movement" and to integrate all the aspects of one's energy. The "calm state" is just an experience, and is not contemplation itself. When one is actually in contemplation, in the state of pure presence, there is then no difference between the calm state and the movement. So there is no need for one to seek a state without thoughts. As Garab Dorje said, "If there does arise [the movement of thoughts], be aware of the state in which they arise. If one is free of thoughts, be aware of the state in which one is free of them. Then there is no difference between the arising of thought

and being free of it." Thus, when one practices contemplation, there is no need to try to find a calm state and avoid
the movement, but one should just maintain one and the
same state of presence in both experiences.

In all the Buddhist traditions of meditation, two phases
are spoken of, namely, meditation on the state of calm or
"shinay," and intuitive vision or "lhanton" *(lhag mthong)*.[8]
Shinay meditation works to bring about a state of mental
calm, in which thoughts no longer have the capacity to disturb the practitioner. Lhanton, on the other hand, is generally taken to mean a kind of inner awakening of consciousness, but it is interpreted differently in the different systems
of the teaching.

In the Sutras it is considered to be an attainment related
to the body, the voice, and the mind, which arises automatically after one has practiced the meditation on the state of
calm. In tantrism, however, it is regarded as a specific level
of realization of the practice of transformation, that manifests as signs linked to the *prana,* the *chakra,* and so on. It
could be said that shinay corresponds to voidness, lhanton
to clarity, and the union of these two is the final arrival point
of the practice of tantra.

But in Dzogchen, in the Series of the Nature of the Mind,
lhanton is a level of the integration of the state of presence
with movement. It is also called the "unchangeable state"
(mi g.yo ba), which cannot be disturbed by any movement.
"Movement" here includes also the energy of the karmic
prana, which usually has a considerable influence on the
mind. In this state, every aspect of the body, voice, and mind
is integrated with contemplation. If a practitioner happens
to be meditating near a noisy machine, he or she has no
need to seek a quiet place instead, because at this stage practice is completely integrated with every type of perception.

The practitioner is no longer obliged to remain tethered to the calm state, but is aware of the karmic dimension of the movement, and does not perceive it as something external to him or herself.

When the levels of progress in contemplation are explained, the images of a stream, a river, and the sea, and so on, are used as examples of the development of the capacity of integration achieved. When a practitioner has attained complete stability in contemplation, even if he is not engaged in any practice in particular, as soon as he falls asleep he finds himself in the state of the natural light,[9] and when he dreams, is aware that he is dreaming. Such an individual's practice is complete, and whether he lives or dies, he is always present, having achieved the Sambhogakaya. When he dies, and the "Bardo of the Essential Condition" (*dharmatā*) manifests, he is ready that very instant to integrate with it in realization.

Chapter Eight
THE FRUIT AND THE WAY OF BEHAVING

Everything has already been accomplished, and so, having overcome the sickness of effort, one finds oneself in the self-perfected state: this is contemplation.

If one has really understood that our real condition is the self-perfected state, then there is a base on which one can develop. If one hasn't understood this, however, even if one studies all the different systems of teachings, one remains in a state of ignorance. From this point of view, even a very learned person could be considered ignorant, while a person without the slightest scholarly education could perfectly well have real knowledge. Study, analysis, philosophic inquiry, and so on, can be useful if one knows how to benefit from them, but often they are an obstacle to true understanding.

Let's take the example of a person who becomes interested in Oriental philosophy because he or she is dissatisfied with Western philosophy. He or she might study and go deeply into the various streams of Oriental thought and then come across Buddhist philosophy, becoming fascinated by its principles. This person then comes to believe that he or she has finally found a valid alternative to his or her own culture. Getting further and further involved, the person then studies and becomes a follower of the philosophy of Nagarjuna, and is completely convinced of the validity of this point of view. But what has in fact happened is that this person has become a slave of the ideology of Nagarjuna, because he or she has now formed an idea, a concept, of voidness, and does not have real knowledge of it, based on real experience. In fact, philosophical convictions and theories, even if they seem perfect, can crumble from one day to the next, because they are based on something fundamentally false, that is to say, on the mind.

The principle in Dzogchen is to avoid creating anything false, and to really understand the reasons for what one is doing. It is not important to define oneself as belonging to this or that school, tradition, or point of view, and it makes no difference whether one considers oneself to be Buddhist or not. Basically, feeling oneself to be a follower of something or other is just a limit, and what one really needs is to understand one's own condition and to open oneself, getting rid of all these kinds of barriers.

In Tibet, during the last century, a tradition arose from the efforts of certain masters who tried to do away with the ideological barriers that had arisen between the various schools, and to favor an openness and exchange of ideas between the different lineages of the teachings. These masters, who originally belonged to various schools, were all great practitioners of Dzogchen, and even if they themselves

Ekajati, the "Maroon-colored Queen,"
main protectress of the Dzogchen teachings

did not define themselves in any way, they were called "nonsectarian" *(ris med)*[1] by others. For a practitioner of Dzogchen, even to call oneself "nonsectarian" is just another way of taking a position of one's own in relation to the position of someone else, which is irrelevant, because the truth is that any definition of this kind at all is an unnecessary limitation.

The primordial state, for example, is defined as being made up of the "three wisdoms," *essence, nature,* and *energy,* but this explanation is only a provisional device intended to help us, caught up as we are in our limits, wandering in continual transmigration, so that we can get an idea of what it is really about. But no analyses or definitions can really encompass the primordial state, and they are only a means suitable to our condition of ignorance.

Jamyang Khyentse Wangpo ('Jam dbyangs mkhyen brtse'i dbang po) and Jamgon Kongtrul ('Jam mgon kong sprul) are said, in the same way, to have been the founders of the nonsectarian tradition we have just spoken of, even though they never had any intention of closing themselves up in a school. When the sun rises in the sky its rays inevitably shine out, but the sun doesn't say, "See how my rays shine!" It's the people who have been in the dark who define the situation by saying, "Look, now there's the light of the sun." So the masters of this tradition, practicing Dzogchen, behaved in a way that was beyond the limits of a sect, without ever taking a position opposed to the sectarian way of seeing things.

There is a Dzogchen saying that goes, "It doesn't get caught up in limits, it doesn't belong to a school," and limits are, in fact, a typical manifestation of dualism, which is the cause of transmigration. Overcoming our limits means discovering the true condition of "what is," and behaving in such a way that our knowledge will actually match the reality of our existence, in all its aspects of body, voice, and mind. This is extremely important. The idea of "nonsectarianism" fundamentally presumes a dualistic separation of oneself and others, which is a barrier that one has to get rid of in order to be able to integrate one's practice with every circumstance in every situation. There are no barriers in the true condition of "what is," and in that condition all tensions are relaxed. Practicing actually means unwinding one's tensions. We talk a lot about overcoming attachment, but what is the source of it? It actually arises from the tensions that we come to create after we have separated our reality into self and other. Thus the only real way to overcome this attachment is to find oneself in a state of relaxed presence. The fact is that an authentic state of presence is, by its very nature, relaxed.

The last two verses of the *Six Vajra Verses* explain the meaning of the *fruit* and the *way of behaving*. In Dzogchen the way one behaves in the state of presence is the fruit, and there is nothing else to obtain. When one has this state of knowledge one discovers that everything was always already accomplished from the very beginning. The self-perfected state is the inherent quality of the condition of "what is"; there is nothing to be perfected, and all one needs to do is to have real knowledge of this condition.

It is not necessary to take up any particular position of the body, or gaze of the eyes, in order to practice, and one should not condition one's existence in any way, but remain in a natural state. Effort and a sense of obligation, which arise from worry and tension, are typical manifestations of the reasoning mind, and in these verses they are compared to a sickness, which, when one has overcome it, gives way to one's finally finding oneself in the dimension of genuine awareness of the state of self-perfection. The real state cannot be created or constructed, but is the true inherent condition of every individual, which is linked to the relative condition of body, voice, and mind. When one has knowledge of this state, without effort, without being confined to limited sessions of practice, our relaxed presence integrates with our whole lives. Thus, our contemplation becomes continuous, and when one reaches this state the qualities of self-perfection, known as the "three bodies," manifest automatically, in the same way that the sun's rays shine out when the sun rises into the sky.

In Dzogchen, the way of behaving is the key to the practice, not because there are fixed rules as to what one should and should not do, but because the principle is that one must learn to become responsible for oneself, working with one's own awareness. But one of the dangers that may be encountered by someone who does not correctly understand what is meant by "not correcting," is that they may just go along with whatever happens, still remaining in a state of distraction. It is said that Padmasambhava gave this advice to his disciples: "With respect to the state of knowledge, follow the way of seeing and the way of practicing Dzogchen. But with respect to the way of behaving, follow the rules of Vinaya." We can be sure that Padmasambhava certainly did not say this because he considered it unimportant for one to learn to be responsible for oneself, but that he said it out of prudence, in order to not give rise to misunderstanding.

Nubchen Sangye Yeshe (gNubs chen sangs rgyas ye shes), a Tibetan master who was a disciple of Padmasambhava, in his treatise called *Light for the Eyes of Meditation (bSam gtan mig sgron)*,[2] said, "Some masters affirm that even if the principle of Dzogchen is that of not correcting anything, one cannot reach this state without correcting. They call what they teach 'Dzogchen,' but practically speaking what they teach is various ways of correcting everything. This is an error; it's like shooting an arrow without knowing what your target is."

It is important, in Dzogchen, to know exactly where one is aiming to arrive at, but at the same time one must not ignore one's own capacity. If one discovers that one's own capacity is not sufficient to enable one to live with awareness, then it would be better to follow some rules until one's awareness is more developed. If, for example, I like to drink but I know that alcohol is bad for me, then I can simply try to stop drinking. But if, as soon as I see a bottle of alcohol, I experience such a strong desire to drink that I can't control myself, this means that I need a precise rule to follow to govern that situation. To recognize this is also part of our awareness.

Dzogchen is said to be a teaching for those with a higher level of capacity. This "higher capacity" means that one has those qualities that are necessary to enable one to understand and apply the teaching. If one lacks any of these qualities, one can try to develop them. In order to give results, awareness must always be accompanied by presence. Being aware means knowing the consequences of one's actions, but sometimes, even though one knows that a certain action will be harmful, one still nevertheless goes ahead and does it, because one is not present in the moment. If one is not present, it makes no difference whether one is aware or not. A person who, in a distracted moment, drinks a cup of poison even though they are aware of its harmful effects, will die in just the same way as another person who lacked that awareness.

It is usually very easy for us to become distracted through our passions, our agitated states of mind, our attachments, and so on. Two people who fall in love, for example, in the first glow of their romance can sometimes hardly bear to be apart even for an instant. They don't realize that they have become distracted and blinded by their passions. After a few weeks, a few months, or a few years, however, their passion begins to grow weaker, and to become "stale." The couple no longer feel at all the same way, and in fact can't bear to be close to one another anymore. Sometimes, in such situations, the relationship can actually go so wrong that the two people begin to hate each other so much that they even come to the point of physical violence. This is an example of how one can become distracted by one's passions.

A Dzogchen practitioner must try to become aware and to understand the real nature of relationships without confusing it with the passions. The relationship between person and person is very important and, especially when it concerns two practitioners, it is essential that each knows how to collaborate with the other without creating problems and obstacles. It is natural for human beings to live as couples rather than to renounce the passions. If two practitioners live together they must not base their relationship on blind passion, because this can have extremely negative consequences. But if the couple understand the essential nature of the passions, then, without either abandoning or underestimating them, they can integrate the passions themselves with their practice.

This is exactly what is meant in tantrism when the transformation of the passions into wisdoms is spoken of. In Dzogchen, if one knows how to enter and remain in the state of "what is," all one's passions, sensations, and so on, can become experiences that will help one to develop one's knowledge. It's not at all true that a practitioner must have no passions, and must become like a rock. In fact, quite the reverse is true; a practitioner must be in full possession of all the manifestations of his or her energy, and, without being distracted by them, must integrate them with contemplation.

The Dzogchen teachings always advise that one tries to help oneself, that one should give oneself a helping hand, as it were. But how, exactly? One should try to always be aware of one's own condition in all the various circumstances one encounters, and if one is either over-agitated or confused, one should try to relax and give oneself space. If one is tired, one should rest. There's no need to follow precise rules, even if, as we have already said, they can sometimes be useful. We need always to remember the goal we are aiming for, which is a way of living our lives with the real presence of awareness.

We need to behave with awareness, too, in our relationship with society, so that the individual's inner development can really evolve to a full maturity. Many political ideologies encourage the individual to engage in a struggle to build a better society. But the way they propose to do this is through overthrowing the old society, perhaps by means of a revolution. In practice, however, the benefits produced by such means are always relative and provisional, and a real equality between social classes is never achieved. The truth is that a better society will only arise through the evolution of the individual. This is because society is made up of millions of individuals. To count to a million, one has to start with number one, which means one has to start with the individual, the only real place one can actually begin to change something. This doesn't mean putting oneself first in an egotistical way, but rather it involves our coming to understand the condition of the whole of humanity through understanding our own experience. With this experience as our guide, we will know how to behave with awareness in any circumstance in every type of society.

We need to know how to work with our situation and with others according to the circumstances that we may encounter, without prejudging or faking anything. Thus, in order to learn how to practice Dzogchen one has to observe oneself. To do this, one only has to pay attention for a few minutes to the way in which our thoughts, our judgments, and our ideas come and go, like waves that arise and disappear. The characteristic nature of our minds is that every thought can be a secondary cause for the carrying out of an action. So if, in our lives, we are aware and present in relation to all aspects of our existence, we will certainly experience less problems.

It is much more important to try to be present and aware at all times rather than just to dedicate a limited period each day to specific practices. Learning the details of techniques of meditation, visualization, and so on, is secondary. There is a saying in Dzogchen which goes, "The principal thing is not meditation but knowledge." And, in fact, if one does not have this knowledge, meditation just becomes a creation of the mind, a superfluous construction. But where does real knowledge come from? It arises from awareness of our existence at the relative level, which is the real basis for an understanding of meditation and the nature of the mind.

This term, "the nature of the mind," may very well be an elegant and fascinating phrase, but the problem is that people don't really know what it means. If we don't actually live in the nature of the mind we only have a mental concept of it, and even though we may speak of it, and think about it, all that has actually nothing whatsoever to do with the reality of it. If we are hungry, for example, it is not enough that we just think, "Eating and not eating are the same thing"; or, "There's no such thing as food at the level of the nature of the mind." It's better if we understand our material situation as it really is. The nature of the mind is a term that refers to a condition that is beyond the existence of the body, the voice, and the mind, the knowledge of which can only arise through experience. Knowing the limits and characteristics of the relative condition one can really become aware of their true nature.

A practitioner must always be aware of the importance of his or her relationship with the master. A master teaches through the three transmissions, direct, symbolic, and oral. But oral transmission doesn't only take place in the moments in which the master is formally seated in a room with hundreds of persons before him, to whom he is explaining various theoretical aspects of the teachings. The master can transmit the state of knowledge at any moment, and any conversation or advice he may give is part of the oral transmission.

If the master finds the stinking body of a dead rat and shows it to the disciple saying, "Smell this stench!"—this might be the means he has chosen to use to transmit knowledge of the state of contemplation. Smelling the stench of a dead rat is a direct, concrete experience, and one in the face of which it is not necessary to pretend or make a great effort actually to have the experience. If, then, through this experience the disciple is able to understand the state in which there is no distinction between a terrible smell and the scent of a rose, the dead rat will have sufficed as a means of transmission. But this is just an example of the infinite variety of situations which the master can use. The teachings are not just something sacred, to be found only in temples and scriptures, they are actually the real understanding of the inherent state of all human experience.

Garab Dorje, the first Dzogchen master, after teaching for the whole of his life, left behind for all the Dzogchen practitioners of the future a small testament, three verses long. The verses read:

> Directly discover your state.
> Don't remain in doubt.
> Gain confidence in self-liberation.[3]

"Directly discovering your state" refers to the transmission by the master, who, in various ways, introduces and brings the disciple to understand the condition of "what is," the individual's primordial state. This is the *base*. "Not remaining in doubt" means that one must have a precise knowledge of this state, finding the state of the presence of contemplation which is one and the same in all the thousands of possible experiences. This is the *path*. "Gain confidence in self-liberation" is the *fruit*. What it means is that the complete and unchangeable knowledge of self-liberation is totally integrated with one's daily life, and that in all circumstances one continues in that state. All the hundreds and hundreds of original texts of Dzogchen can be considered to be an explanation of these three verses of Garab Dorje. But the teachings are not just a book or a tradition, they are a living state of knowledge.

NOTES AND REFERENCES

Editor's Introduction

1. I have given the exact transliteration of Tibetan terms in italics within parentheses the first time the term is used.

2. In ancient times the term "Bon" was used in Tibet to refer to any type of ritual tradition based on the recitation of mantras or magic formulae, which probably did not differ greatly from the various forms of shamanism widespread in Central Asia. Later, at the time of the appearance on the scene of the master Tonpa Shenrab (sTon pa gShen rab), born in 1917 BC according to Bon sources, many of these ritual traditions were perfected and linked up by a common conception in which existence is understood as a process of interdependence between the individual's energy and external energies dominated by various classes of beings. Again according to Bon sources, Tonpa Shenrab, who originally came from Shang-shung (western Tibet), taught the sciences of medicine and astrology and an early form of Dzogchen. It was only in the period between the eighth and the ninth centuries AD that Bon, threatened with extinction because of the growing spread of Buddhism, began to clothe itself in a philosophical and doctrinal structure, influenced by the principles of Buddhism themselves. From this period on Bon "became" a religion, and, in its general

characteristics, could no longer be clearly distinguished from the other Buddhist schools.

3. According to the texts of the Series of Secret Instructions of Dzogchen, Garab Dorje was born 360 years after the *parinirvana* of the Buddha, in 184 BC. On the other hand, according to the *Vairo rgyud 'bum*, the collection of works translated into Tibetan by Vairochana, Garab Dorje's birth took place twenty-eight years after the Buddha's passing, which would make the date 516 BC. This latter date would confirm the tradition which has it that Garab Dorje was the son of the Princess of Oddiyana, Praharini, daughter of King Indrabhuti, who discovered Padmasambhava on Lake Dhanakosha eight years after the parinirvana of the Buddha.

4. This tradition is based on the lineage of masters set down in the Series of Secret Instructions of Dzogchen. However, according to the lineage documented in the Series of the Nature of the Mind, which has more historical credibility, Shri Singha lived much later than Manjushrimitra. Thus, it seems more reasonable to suppose that the transmission from Manjushrimitra to Shri Singha took place by means of visions and contacts of an extraordinary nature.

5. During the second spread of Buddhism in Tibet several new tantras were introduced, and some of those introduced at the time of Padmasambhava were retranslated. It was during this period that the other schools of Tibetan Buddhism were formed: the Kagyudpa (*bKa' rgyud pa*), the Sakyapa (*Sa skya pa*), and the Kadampa (*bKa' gdams pa*), which latter, when later reformed, became known as the Gelugpa (*dGe lugs pa*).

6. I have rendered the term *sems* (mind) as "the nature of the mind," because in all the ancient Dzogchen writings *sems* is used as an abbreviation of *byang chub kyi sems* (*bodhicitta*), the primordial nature of the mind.

7. Termas can be subdivided into two categories: "sater" (*sa gter*), "treasures of the earth," which are both objects and manuscripts actually found buried in the earth; and "gonter" (*dgongs gter*), "treasures of the state of knowledge," which are texts memorized in the basic consciousness of an individual, that can be recalled

spontaneously in the state of contemplation, even many incarnations after the original memorization.

8. Shang-shung (Zhang zhung), the area that was the original source of Tibetan culture, once actually included the whole of Tibet. With its capital in Khyunlun Nulkar (Khyung lung ngul mkhar), near Mount Kailash, Shang-shung was subdivided into three regions: internal, corresponding to western Tibet; central, corresponding to central Tibet; and external, including eastern Tibet and the areas on the border with China. When the little independent kingdom of Yarlung in central Tibet began to expand and to conquer the surrounding areas during the reign of King Songtsen Gampo (Srong btsan sgam po) (617-698 AD), Shang-shung itself was also annexed. In this way the whole kingdom came to be called Tibet (*Bod*). The religion of Shang-shung was Bon, and its priests had great political influence at court.

9. His paternal uncle, rTogs ldan O rgyan bstan 'dzin (1893-1959), and his maternal uncle, 'Jam dbyangs Chos kyi dbang phyug (1910-1963).

10. One of his teachings on Mahamudra can be found in C.C. Chang, *Teachings of Tibetan Yoga* (Hyde-Park: University Books, 1963).

11. These include: *The Necklace of Gzi: A Cultural History of Tibet* (Dharamsala: Information Office of H.H. the Dalai Lama, 1981).

PART ONE

Chapter One
The Individual: Body, Voice, and Mind

1. A work by Vasubandhu, an Indian master, on Buddhist metaphysics.

2. *Tsampa* is roasted barley flour, which is mixed with Tibetan tea and butter. It is the staple diet of the Tibetan people.

3. The fifth Dalai Lama, Blo bzang rgya mtsho (1617-1682), was also a "terton" (*gter ston*), a discoverer of terma, or hidden texts.

4. Yantra Yoga (*'phrul khor*) is the Buddhist equivalent of Hatha Yoga, from which it is distinguished by the dynamics of its movements and the particular importance given to breathing. There were several different types of Yantra Yoga in Tibet, traditionally linked to specific tantric practices. Namkhai Norbu, for many years, has himself taught a system of Yantra Yoga that dates back to the master Vairochana.

Chapter 2
The Paths of Renunciation and of Transformation

1. In tantrism, method (*upāya; thabs*) and energy (*prajñā; shes rab*) are considered to be the two fundamental principles of existence, corresponding to male and female, or solar and lunar energies. *Prajñā* (superior knowledge) in this context is synonymous with "energy."

2. The five aggregates (*skandha*) are a fundamental concept of Buddhist psychology. They are: form, sensation, perception, volition, and consciousness. See C. Trungpa, *Glimpses of Abhidharma* (Boston: Shambhala Publications).

3. The five passions are: anger, attachment, mental obscuration, pride, and jealousy.

4. The five Buddhas are the Sambhogakaya manifestations of the individual's own condition. The five wisdoms are functions linked to aspects of the five basic elements: space, air, water, earth, and fire. For their names, and the correct correspondences, see K. Dowman, *Skydancer* (London: Routledge and Kegan Paul, 1984) p. 178.

5. The *Kalachakra Tantra* is considered to have been taught by Buddha Sakyamuni, at the age of eighty-one, at the Dhanyakataka stupa in southern India.

6. The five wisdom activities are: pacifying action, for purification, corresponding to the element water, the easterly direction, and the colour white; wrathful action, for overcoming negative energies, corresponding to the element air, the northerly direction, and the colour green; powerful action, for conquering,

corresponding to the element fire, the westerly direction, and the colour red; the action of growth, for prosperity, corresponding to the element earth, the southerly direction, and the colour yellow.

7. *Chakra*, literally "wheels," are the principal points in which energy concentrates in the human body. One visualizes four, five, six, or seven chakra, according to the different methods used in different tantras. *Nadi* are subtle, nonmaterial channels through which energy circulates in all parts of the body.

8. The Anuttara-tantras are classed as Father Tantras when the practice given greater importance is the development stage; as Mother Tantras when the perfectioning stage is more important; and Nondual when the two phases of practice are given equal importance.

9. The term "divinity" is a partial and imprecise translation of *yi dam*, which literally means "sacred mind." In tantrism, the "divinity" is a manifestation of the pure dimension of the individual him or herself, and not something external. The wrathful form of the "divinity" represents the dynamic nature of energy; the joyful form represents the sensation of pleasure; and the peaceful form represents the calm state of mind, without thoughts.

Chapter Three
The Path of Self-Liberation

1. Samantabhadra (Kun tu bzang po), the primordial Buddha, is the symbol of the state of the Dharmakaya. He is represented as being naked, without ornaments, and blue in color, to show the purity of the *essence*, and the depth of the void.

2. The cycle of sutras known as the *Prajñāpāramitā*, the high point of the Mahayana teachings, is considered to be a revelation of Nagarjuna, the famous Indian master who was the founder of the Madhyamika or Middle Way system of philosophy.

3. To understand correctly the concept of voidness, the examples are given in the Sutras of the "rabbit's horn" and the "bull's horn." There has never been such a thing as a rabbit's horn, and so it would be useless to deny its existence. If we were to deny the

existence of a bull's horn, on the other hand, we would be directly denying the existence of something whose existence we consider real and material. In the same way the "void" is not an attribute of an "abstract condition" of things, but is the very nature of their materiality.

4. *Thugs rje ma' gags pa.* In many Western translations the term *thugs rje,* in a Dzogchen context, has been rendered as "compassion." According to the explanation given by Namkhai Norbu, this is an imprecise and partial interpretation of the term. *Thugs* means "the state of the mind," and *rje* means "lord." What is being referred to is in fact energy, which is the manifestation of the primordial state. In the sutras, compassion is considered to be the energy of the void, and thus it is also called *thugs rje.* But in Dzogchen, compassion is regarded as being only one of the many aspects of energy.

5. See: N. Norbu, ed., *Il Libro Tibetano dei Morti* (Rome: Newton Compton, 1979); F. Freemantle and C. Trungpa, *The Tibetan Book of the Dead* (Berkeley: Shambhala Publications, 1975); G. Orofino, ed., *Insegnamenti Tibetani su Morte e Liberazione* (Rome: Edizioni Mediterranee, 1985), published in English as *Sacred Tibetan Teachings on Death and Liberation* by Prism Unity Press, 1990.

6. *Rig pa* is one of the key terms in the Dzogchen teachings. Its literal meaning is "knowledge," but the accepted use of the term in Dzogchen expresses much more than that. It refers to the intuitive and direct knowledge of the primordial condition, maintained as a living presence. In this book I have rendered the term *rig pa* as "the state of presence," and sometimes as just "presence," although I have used this word also to render the Tibetan *dran pa,* which refers more specifically to presence of mind.

7. The term Nirmanakaya generally also denotes the manifestation of a realized being, who, in order to give teachings, assumes a human form, or the form of another type of being. Buddha Shakyamuni, Padmasambhava, and Garab Dorje, for example, are considered to be Nirmanakaya manifestations.

8. The *Abhisamayalankara* is a work of Asanga, an important Indian philosopher of the Mahayana tradition.

9. gYung ston rdo rje dpal (1284-1365).

Chapter Four
The Importance of Transmission

1. Tapihritsa is one of the most important masters of the lineage of the *Oral Tradition of the Dzogchen of Shang-shung (rDzogs pa chen po zhang zhung snyan brgyud)*, which contains what are in fact the most ancient Bon teachings, even though they did not come to be written down until the seventh century AD.

2. The methods of practice that lead to the realization of the Body of Light are principally *thod rgal* and *yang tig*, which are contained in the Series of Secret Instructions. The state of contemplation is the basis of these practices.

3. Vajrasattva, depicted as smiling, white in colour, with silk ornaments and vajra and bell in his hands, represents the Sambhogakaya. Vajrasattva practice is particularly effective for purification.

4. For examples of parables and riddles in ancient Dzogchen writings see N. Norbu, *Drung, Deu and Bon* (Dharamsala: Library of Tibetan Works and Archives, 1995).

5. Tilopa (988-1069 AD) and Naropa (1016-1100 AD) are the first two masters of a lineage which later included Marpa and Milarepa, and from which the Kagyudpa tradition arose.

6. Vajra Kilaya is one of the eight cycles of tantric divinities introduced to Tibet by Padmasambhava.

7. Yeshe Tsogyel (Ye shes mtsho rgyal) was the principal consort and disciple of Padmasambhava. Her biography has been translated in Keith Dowman, *Skydancer* (London: Routledge and Kegan Paul, 1984).

8. A *damaru* is a little two-sided drum used in tantric rituals. Sometimes it is made of a human skull.

9. Dzogchen texts are called "Tantras" even though they do not contain teachings of the path of transformation, because they explain the nature of the individual's primordial state, which is a "continuation" (*tantra*) of the manifestation of energy.

10. What are referred to here are revealed texts known as "treasures of the state of knowledge."

11. Nyag bla Pad ma bdud 'dul (1816-1872).

12. *Ganapuja* is a tantric ritual, made up of various phases, whose aim is the reconfirming of the "promise" or commitment (*samaya*) between the disciple and the master, and also between disciple and disciple. In addition to this, through consuming food and drink in the ganapuja, the practitioners develop their capacity to integrate contemplation with the sense-pleasures, as well as entering into the state beyond dualism, which is the inner meaning of the samaya.

13. The Chod (*gcod*) is a practice based on offering one's own body, in a visualized form, to the spirits and other beings who cause disturbances and hindrances, to pacify them and to pay one's karmic debts to them. The Chod is chanted to the accompaniment of the damaru and bell. Originally based on the principle of "voidness" found in the Prajñaparamita, this practice was developed and perfected by the great Tibetan lady master Machig Labdron (Ma gcig lab sgron) (1031-1129).

14. For the biography of this extraordinary practitioner, who was considered to be a living dakini, see T. Allione, *Women of Wisdom* (London: Routledge and Kegan Paul, 1984).

15. gTsang pa grub chen was one of the principal masters of Namkhai Norbu's uncle, mKhyen brtse Chos kyi dbang phyug (1910-1963).

16. This uncle was called rTogs ldan O rgyan bstan 'dzin. According to recent reports from Tibet, he too realized the Body of Light.

17. rDo grub chen 'Jigs med bstan pa'i nyi ma (1865-1926), third reincarnation of rDo grub chen 'Jigs med phrin las 'od zer (1745-1821), direct disciple of the great master 'Jigs med gling pa.

PART TWO

Introduction

1. The subdivision of the Dzogchen writings into tantras (*rgyud*), "lung" (*lung*), or literally, "quotations," and secret instructions (*man ngag*) is being referred to here. While the first two of these three categories contain teachings originally transmitted by Garab Dorje, the third contains instructions and explanations that derive from the experience of various masters.

2. Tradition has it that it was Padmasambhava himself who suggested to King Trisong Detsen that he send Vairochana to Oddiyana.

3. There exists a "Tantra of the Cuckoo" with this title in the *rNying ma'i rgyud 'bum*, the canon of Nyingmapa scriptures.

4. The documents found at Tun Huang, which is situated in Chinese Turkestan, were discovered at the beginning of this century by A. Stein and P. Pelliot. Thanks to the sandy nature of the soil in Tun Huang, which was once an outpost of the Tibetan empire, manuscripts of immense value to the study of Tibetan history and culture were preserved for posterity.

Chapter Six
The Base and the Way of Seeing

1. In Tibetan: *bde ba, gsal ba,* and *mi rtog pa.*

2. Namkhai Norbu was recognized as the reincarnation of Ngag dbang rnam rgyal (1594-1651), the founder of the state of Bhutan, and of A 'dzom 'brug pa (1842-1934), a great master of Dzogchen, who was the master of, among others, Changchub Dorje.

3. The text here referred to is the *Aspiration to the Base, Path, and Fruit (gZhi lam 'bras bu'i smon lam)*, contained in the *kLong chen*

snying thig, the famous terma revealed by 'Jigs med gling pa (1729-98).

Chapter Seven
The Path and the Way of Practicing

1. The *Great Space of Vajrasattva* (*rDo rje sems dpa' nam mkha' che*) is a text belonging to the category of *lung*, which, it is said, was first transmitted by Garab Dorje when he was a child, at which time he recited it spontaneously.

2. *Cog bzhag rnam pa bzhi*, the four ways of "leaving it without correcting it," are: "like a mountain" (*ri bo cog bzhag*), linked to the body; "like the ocean" (*rgya mtsho cog bzhag*), linked to the eyes; "of the state of presence" (*rig pa cog bzhag*); and "of vision" (*snang ba cog bzhag*), which is based on the principle of the integration of all one's sense perceptions.

3. The Buddhist rosary, with 108 beads.

4. This verse is, in Tibetan, made up of the names of Vairochana (rNam par snang mdzad), one of the five Sambhogakaya Buddhas, and Samantabhadra (Kun tu bzang po), the symbol of the dharmakaya.

5. *Thogs bcas kyi bdud.* The other three demons which impede the practitioner's progress are: "The devil which does not block" (*thogs med*), which relates to one's thoughts; "the devil of pleasure" (*dga' brod*), which involves attachment to the results of one's practice; and "the devil of the ego principle" (*snyem byed*).

6. This refers to the "vase initiation" (*bum dbang*), whose aim is to purify the obstacles of the body.

7. The refuge vow is the foundation of Buddhist practice in all traditions, whether for monks or for lay people. The objects of refuge are the Buddha, the teaching (*dharma*), and the spiritual community (*sangha*), called the "three jewels." At the tantric level, however, the objects of refuge are the master (*guru*), the divinity (*deva*), and the *ḍākinī*.

8. In Sanskrit, *śamatha* and *vipaśyanā*.

9. The state of the natural light (*'od gsal*) corresponds to the phase between one's falling asleep and the arising of dreams. In this period, even if the mind does not function, the practitioner continues in the clarity of the state of presence.

Chapter Eight
The Fruit and the Way of Behaving

1. This arose in eastern Tibet, as a result of the work of two great masters, 'Jam dbyangs mkhyen brtse'i dbang po (1820-92) and 'Jam mgon kong sprul (1813-1899).

2. This text, the work of Nubchen Sangye Yeshe (ninth century), reviews the characteristics of all the Buddhist traditions, including Ch'an or Zen and tantrism, in relation to the Dzogchen teachings. Because of this, it is of extreme importance as a means to understanding the differences of view and practice between Dzogchen and the other schools during the period of the first spread of Buddhism in Tibet.

3. In Tibetan: *ngo rang thog tu 'phrad/ thag gcig thog tu bcad/ bdengs grol thog tu 'cha'*.

PUBLICATIONS BY CHÖGYAL NAMKHAI NORBU

'The Biography of A-Yu Khadro, Dorje Paldron', written by Namkhai Norbu, in: *Women of Wisdom,* by Tsultrim Allione, published by Routledge and Kegan Paul, London, 1984.

The Crystal and the Way of Light. Sutra, Tantra, and Dzogchen, The Teachings of Namkhai Norbu, compiled and edited by John Shane, published by Penguin Arkana, New York and London, 1986.

The Cycle of Day and Night, Where One Proceeds Along the Path of the Primordial Yoga. A basic text on the practice of Dzogchen, translated and edited by John Reynolds, published by Station Hill Press, New York, 1987.

Dream Yoga and the Practice of Natural Light, edited and introduced by Michael Katz, Snow Lion Publications, Ithaca, New York, USA, 1992.

Drung, Deu, and Bon: Narrations, Symbolic Languages, and the Bon Tradition in Ancient Tibet, translated from Tibetan into Italian and edited by Adriano Clemente, translated into English by Andrew Lukianowicz, published by the Library of Tibetan Works and Archives, Dharamsala, 1995.

Dzogchen and Zen, edited and with a Preface and Notes by Kennard Lipman, published by Zhang Zhung Editions, Oakland, California, 1984.

Il Libro Tibetano dei Morti, translation into Italian of *The Tibetan Book of the Dead,* published by Newton Comton Editori, Rome, 1983.

A Journey into the Culture of Tibetan Nomads, in Tibetan with an Introduction in English, published by Shang-Shung Edizioni, Merigar, 58031 Arcidosso, GR, Italy.

The Mirror, Advice on Presence and Awareness, translated from Tibetan into Italian by Adriano Clemente, and from Italian into English by John Shane, published by Shang-Shung Edizioni, Merigar, 58031 Arcidosso, GR, Italy, 1983.

The Necklace of Gzi, A Cultural History of Tibet, published by the Information Office of His Holiness the Dalai Lama, Dharamsala, India, 1981. Tibetan and English editions.

On Birth and Life, A Treatise on Tibetan Medicine, translated from Tibetan into Italian by Namkhai Norbu and Enrico Dell'Angelo, and from Italian into English by Barrie Simmons, published by Shang-Shung Edizioni, Merigar, 58031 Arcidosso, GR, Italy.

Primordial Experience: An Introduction to rDzogs-chen Meditation, a text by Manjusrimitra, translated by Namkhai Norbu and Kennard Lipman, with the collaboration of Barrie Simmons, published by Shambhala Publications, Boston and London, 1987.

Rigbay Kujyug: The Six Vajra Verses, edited by Cheh-Ngee Goh, published by Rinchen Editions, Singapore, 1990.

The Small Collection of Hidden Precepts. A Study of an Ancient Manuscript of Dzogchen from Tun-Huang, a study of a text by Buddhagupta, with a commentary by Namkhai Norbu and an extensive glossary of Dzogchen terms, published by Shang-Shung Edizioni, Merigar, 58031 Arcidosso, GR, Italy.

Yantra Yoga: Yoga of Movement, edited by Oliver F. Leik, published by Edition Tsaparang, Austria, 1988.

Many other specialized publications by Chögyal Namkhai Norbu in English and other languages are available from: Shang-Shung Edizioni, c/o Merigar, 58031 Arcidosso, GR, Italy. Write for a list.

THE DZOGCHEN COMMUNITY

Principal Seats of the Dzogchen Community

ARGENTINA
  Tashigar, Mariano Moreno 382
  5000 Cordoba

AUSTRALIA
  Namgyalgar, P.O. Box 14
  Central Tilda, 2546 New South Wales

EUROPE
  Merigar, 58031 Arcidosso, GR, Italy

USA
  Tsegyelgar, P.O. Box 227, Conway, MA 01341

Addresses for Dzogchen Communities in many other countries, as well as secondary Dzogchen Communities in the USA, can be obtained by writing to Tsegyelgar.

Newsletter for the Dzogchen Community

The Dzogchen Community publishes a bi-monthly newspaper, *The Mirror*, available from Tsegyelgar.

Index of Tibetan and Sanskrit Terms